His Word, My Encouragement

By: Ashley Reynolds

His Word, My Encouragement
By: Ashley Reynolds

Published by J. Elaine Writes
www.jelainewrites.com

Edited by: J. Elaine Writes
Cover Design by: Design X MEV

This document is published by J.Elaine Writes located in the United States of America. It is protected by the United States Copyright Act, all applicable state laws and international copyright laws.

Printed in the United States of America
ISBN: 978-1-7332352-2-8

Table of Contents

Dedication

Wow! What can I say? Around October of 2018 I began to write out my thoughts. Words became sentences. My sentences turned into paragraphs. My paragraphs then formed a book. I would like to thank My Lord and personal Savior, Jesus Christ for enabling me to finish what was started. I want to dedicate this book to my mother, Pastor Sylvia, for always being so sweet and my personal teddy bear. Your love and encouragement through this entire process has been most appreciated and uplifting. To my dad, Minister Reynolds, who at times can't see the "why's" to what I do, but then in the end understands, thank you for helping me along the way with your many texts and messages of how to handle my business. I would like to dedicate this book to my blood brother, Brother Cone, for fighting through many of the hard and difficult challenges of life. The world hasn't heard your story but one day they will. I also would like to appreciate Prophet J. Davis for answering the call of the Lord on your life to start a publishing company. The level of excellence and expertise is what this generation needs. May the Lord continuously establish the works of your hands. Last, but not least, I dedicate this book to all of those who are just dealing with life and the loudness that it produces at times. With all the demands and unfavorable situations that it can present; I say to you beloved – LISTEN! Listen out for his Words and in doing so, will you be encouraged throughout your journey. God bless you all.

iii

Forward

It's in pain or storms that you will know your true friend, Jesus Christ. It's in the storm that you will be able to know what God is saying about you, your family, marriage, business and ministry. Always remember this.... The pain or storm you are going through is a tool that God uses to push you in to your destiny; this is to say God will allow you to go through pain, persecution, rejection, and gossip as a means of testing you to make you qualify for the upper level or position that you ask of Him. Ruth went through pain, but God favored her in the eyes of Boaz. While in pain or storms, always understand Romans 8:28. All things worketh for good to them that loves the Lord. Revelation 24:1- He will wipe all the tears from them... This is to say we shall pass through the pain, but the good thing is God will be with us. In the book, *His Word, My Encouragement*, Prophetess Ashley uses a compilation of life situations that are common to mankind and encourages us through them all with God's Word. I trust that you will be as blessed by this piece of writing as I was. Blessings unto all.

Pastor Fräncis Mäkomere
Grace Community Fellowship

Abstract

We fight hard to keep a positive outlook on life. However, negative life situations have a way of navigating our minds to the menial things of this life. This epidemic only leads to a lower self-perspective thus causing us to miss the beauty of living on earth. *HIS Word MY ENCOURAGEMENT* is a short, simple book with a myriad of biblical and real-life experiences that most people go through but are too afraid to deal with, let alone talk about. In the book *His Word, My Encouragement*, you will find some helpful biblical strategies on how to gain control of your thoughts concerning negative experiences and to turn them into your everyday advantage.

~ Ashley Reynolds

Chapter 1

Interrupted

Every individual that we read about in the Bible had the trajectory of their lives interrupted. While browsing through the Facebook page of Bishop S.Y. Younger I came across a post that he stated: "If you're called by God then your life will be inconvenienced by God." This direct quote settled in my spirit for some time which began the development of other thoughts. The prophet Amos came to mind. I thought of the parallel of his life as well as my own life after reading the first couple of chapters of his book. Amos was a person who was set on what he should be in this life. However, the prophet came face to face with God's truth about him and God's plan for his life. Though settled with being a shepherd and content with being a keeper of sycamore trees, God's idea of how his days on earth should be spent was greater. Not to say that his time spent caring for sycamore trees and being a shepherd was of no effect. I have always believed that whatever we did before being called into ministry was one of the strategic methods that God would use to prepare us for our "real" purpose in life. Of course, it is not until we surrender over into God's plan for our lives that we will really see this truth at work. Out of nowhere, God began sharing His heart and mind concerning the condition of several countries with Amos. Can you imagine living your life quite normal and then suddenly because God had a need in the kingdom, he chooses you. In the book of Amos, you will find that a prophetically inexperienced shepherd is being exposed early on to prophesy. Say what God? I could only imagine that this was Amos's response. The process that I was exposed to was that you were trained first and then prophesied later. This was to ensure the security of the church and to protect the integrity of the prophetic. In other words, it was to be this way so that the inexperienced prophet would not hurt people with words of truth. There is a certain timing, way, as well as, a certain spirit that one must have to release God's word. Amen, somebody! However, this method was not so with Amos. God just interrupted his life and told him to go do what "mature" prophets would do on a regular basis, which was to prophesy.

Amos 7:14-15,

"Amos answered Amaziah, "I was neither a prophet nor the son of a prophet, but I was a shepherd, and I also took care of sycamore-fig trees. But the Lord took me from tending the flock and said to me, 'Go, prophesy to my people Israel."

It is not that strange how God chose to deal with him on a level that He dealt with prophets that had been trained for 10 plus years. My spiritual trainer at the time would often admit how she felt that it was unfair how God would reveal heavy secretive things with me so early in the prophetic. I would look at her and think if you only knew how I felt about it. I would pray about myself and God would reveal others to me. I was not on my knees praying to see into other people's business, but God would help me with controlling my tongue while releasing what was revealed. I prayed that He would keep me steady in him. I prayed for me. God would deal with me concerning disasters such as people's death, destruction, perverted acts, lying tongues, etc. Yes, I was only in my youth and then in my late teens would it intensify. What was I to do? What was Amos to do? Immediately God started talking to him about the displeasing conditions of such countries as Aram, Philistine, Tyre, Edom, Ammon, Moab, Judah, and Israel. The word of the Lord had always ended in God's "final judgment " of these places, which was gloom and doom. What a heavy weight from the Lord. Then just when you felt that it might get a little lighter for Amos, the Lord began giving Amos woes and visions of doom concerning Israel. It got so bad until the Priest would ask him to go somewhere else to prophesy. You may ask why? It was too heavy. It wasn't that what Amos was saying was not the truth. The people knew that what Amos was saying they were found guilty of, but they would rather remain the same than to be faced with their folly. At this moment I feel impressed that this is one of the most difficult seasons for prophets of the Lord. The Lord is speaking his truth to them all over this world, yet because of the condition of the church, many are not being received. If it's not a word of wealth, promotion or self-gratification then it's not being received. Many are being made a mockery and taken lightly. Such were with the prophets of old. These do not have a word that would gratify the flesh but rather a word

that would challenge this old sinful nature.
However, as I look around in today's church
set up, I become appalled at the level of
perversion, greed, corrupt and disrespect
that we have allowed. If you do not have a
certain look, know certain people or have
certain things then you are rejected and
deemed as not "having it." Like with Amos,
the Lord had released a word which carried
the power to put the church back on track
with God, but the people in high places keep
stifling their voices. That's right, they are
sending them away with intent to shut down
the real prophetic sound that God has sent to
be a real blessing to that region. But as I sit,
I feel strongly that God is about to restore
the true voices for this dispensation. God is
raising up corrected voices again and
nothing by any means will be able to shut
them down.

Amos: 7:12-13, 16,

*"Then Amaziah said to Amos, "Get out, you
seer! Go back to the land of Judah. Earn
your bread there and do your prophesying
there. 13 Don't prophesy anymore at Bethel,
because this is the king's sanctuary and the
temple of the kingdom. 16 Now then, hear
the word of the Lord. You say, "'Do not*

prophesy against Israel, and stop preaching against the descendants of Isaac."

I can only imagine the confusion that Amos felt about his new experience as a prophet. This was all new to Amos, but he had a charge from the Lord and had to rise to the occasion. I feel led through the word of God to let someone know that if you are a prophet/seer and you are under heavy attacks, it's only because you see, and you have great precision and depth in your vision. It's not you that they are coming up against, it is the word of the Lord that has been revealed to you. It's what's in your eye gate that the enemy wants to discourage your spirit so that you are too damaged to go forth. But I say, Go forth prophet!!! That's right open wide your mouth and declare the plans and purposes of our God as commanded. PROPHESY!!!

You may ask in what way does Amos's life and my life parallel. Like Amos, I had already figured out what direction my life should go in. Ever since the 3rd grade, I had always dreamed of being a nurse. My mother is a nurse, one of my grandmothers is a nurse, some of my aunts are nurses and some of my older cousins were nurses. In the light of my understanding, I held on to my truth that in order for me to be deemed a "success" I needed to be a nurse. This way I would be able to have a good income, have a 401K plan, pay a good tithe and be independent. I needed to be like the others in my family in order to be accepted and to be held in high esteem. I had lived down the street from my Pastor. It was only a few days after my high school graduation when I decided to ride with my mother to Pastor's home. We pulled into the driveway and my mom went into the house while I stayed outside to watch the running car. After a short while, my mother and Pastor had come out of the house and my Pastor yelled, "Hey... what are you in that car meditating upon?" I laughed and replied, "Not a thing." The pastor then said, "What the Lord say?" I thought and said, "What did He say about what?" Pastor replied, "About school. What is the Lord saying about school?" I then got out of the car and proudly stated, "Oh... I had a dream of being a doctor. Yes, a gynecologist at that." Lol... Little did I know that those were my plans from a little girl in elementary school. To do something in the medical field was my goal. I have read some articles on the dream realm and found out that if you highly desire to do something then it can start to invade your dream world. Little did I know that I would begin a long journey of finding what God wanted me to do and be over the course of time. Like Amos, I had thought that I was on the path of the Lord but found out that there was another route. Unlike Amos, I had known that the hand of the Lord was upon my life, but I had always thought that I should pick a profession to provide for myself. First, I never wanted to depend on people to provide for me. After all, we know that people can be fickle. However, we also know that at the end of any decision God's plan will prevail.

I remember while attending Oral Roberts University I had met an older lady by the name of Ms. Jann. I remember feeling a little discouraged because I was getting older and had not obtained my degree by that time. Amos had gone from being a shepherd to a herdsman of cattle, to tending sycamore-fig trees. Looks like Amos was on an occupational journey as well. I had gone from being a Pre-Med major, to nursing, to a teaching major. I was both tired and disappointed. However, I was coming from the library and bumped into Mrs. Jann. She and I began to talk about life and one thing that Ms. Jann said to me that day was, "Ashley, no time spent studying and preparing yourself for your future is considered time lost or wasted. Sometimes God spends a longer time on some than others." Those words lifted my spirit and stayed with me throughout the remainder of my time at Oral Robert University. I had the wrong perspective about my long journey in school. God sent Ms. Jann to help me know that my labor was not in vain and that I should praise God that at least I was on the right path now.

The point of this section was to briefly share with you that like Amos we may feel as if we have our journeys mapped out. However, when God steps in to interrupt your plans it may not make sense. It may be a hard thing to allow but God will give the strength needed in the season of letting go. Like Amos, I was on a path and felt comfortable studying in the medical field. However, when he put me in a dream, and I heard, "teacher education and teach my people," I had to surrender. I want to tell you that though I surrendered it was still a journey that had many bumpy roads. However, it was a road worth taking. Many people feel like because they say yes to God's will that everything is going to be easy. To be honest it seemed like things got worse. As a matter of fact, it seems like every time I have decided to follow God's voice things would get worse before I would see that it was really him that told me to do it. This is where many people get tricked and discouraged. It is when this happens that many start to feel that they have missed God and if not careful immature or fleshly voices will try to convince you that you are "off" and somehow need to get back on track. At this moment of your obedient walk, you will need to only allow "right voices" into your ear. These are people who really have a revelation about where you are in your walk with God for your life. When Abram in the bible left out to start his journey with the Lord all he had was a word from the Lord. On a word did he set out to be obedient. Right after He left the bible says that he went into a famine. Not only did he enter a famine, but he also had to go down into Egypt.

Genesis 12:10,

Now there was a famine in the land, and Abram went down to Egypt to live there for a while because the famine was severe.

He didn't go up into Egypt, but he had to go down. There was a retraction. Sometimes when we step out on God's word, we will be highly challenged in our faith to believe God on every word that he has spoken. However, after he went down in the process, he was able to come up with bountiful blessings later. Going back to Amos, he had to take the journey of faith with God to teach him how to operate as a prophet of God but in the end, would God trust him to go further with prophesying to priests and leaders of nations. I started out on one path but got shifted onto another path. As a result of my trust in the Lord, I have completed 4 degrees and soon will pursue a doctorate by the grace of the Lord.

Prayer:

Father in Jesus' name, I thank you for how you have an undeniable plan for my life. Father, according to your word you have good thoughts and plans for me to prosper and to have an expected end. You declared over all who would believe that we could prosper and be in good health even as our soul prospers. Father, just like Amos who was on another path and his life was shifted for a greater purpose, Father we believe that our lives too have been shifted for a better cause. I thank you that when the enemy comes to infiltrate my mind with negative thoughts about the good moves you have made in my life that I will immediately recognize it and put it under the blood of Jesus Christ. I thank you for the ability to accept what you allow and to embrace the life that you have for me in my future. I am victorious. In Jesus' name, amen!

Chapter 2

A Small Place

Amos 1:1

The words of Amos, who was among the herdsmen of Tekoa, which he saw concerning Israel in the days of Uzziah king of Judah...

Amos was a native of Tekoa, which was south of Jerusalem. He was from the southern Kingdom of Judah but preached in the northern Kingdom of Israel. Tekoa was a small district. According to some theologians it could not have been any bigger than a small prosperous village. There in this small village I am sure that Amos' job was very important and contributed highly to the development and promotion of what Tekoa had to offer. Though an intricate voice, I do not believe that Amos was the loudest voice at that time. The amazing thing is that when God needed a prophet to speak on his behalf, He didn't go to the largest rural areas and neither did He investigate the large cities for some popular well-off person. God looked in a small place to find the perfect voice for the

God assignment. Often the choices that God makes are usually, opposite of what man would choose. It would make sense for God to choose someone that had a strong voice in the community, was held in high esteem by the people and well trained to do such a task for him. However, He did not. Why? God's ways are so much higher than ours are.

Isaiah 55:8-9,

"For my thoughts are not your thoughts, neither are your ways my ways, saith the LORD. For as the heavens are higher than the earth, so are my ways higher than your ways, and my thoughts than your thoughts."

In my prayer time, I had gotten through reading one book of the bible and saw an illustration in my mind. I saw a person that was working diligently. This person was minding their business, doing well to others and striving to be a good citizen. In the blink of my eye, I saw everything change. Their clothes changed from that of a pauper to that of royalty. The status of their life changed instantly. I thought in my mind, "Lord what is this and what is its meaning?" The Lord helped my understanding to know that when He has a need in the kingdom He will interrupt one's life drastically without warning. It is only because there is a need. This is one reason no one can boast in themselves because the grace to do anything ultimately comes from God our Father. God knows what He has deposited within all of us and at any moment will He impede our plans for the sake of getting a job carried out in the earth and in heaven. Heaven is backing you up when you say yes to the assignment of God. This requires a great amount of trust. It summons a trust beyond your understanding. It must be confusing when you have become used to living one way and then suddenly you are walking on a path that you are not familiar with. Most people become so adapted to living low until they self-sabotage when elevation comes. We at times fail to realize that just because it's unfamiliar does not mean that it is not where we should be. It is a path that God uses to introduce you to yourself as well as to another level of faith that one would need to grab hold to in order to make it through this new phase of life. When you transition from going from having a menial job, menial responsibility and menial status to suddenly having a gigantic position with God, gigantic responsibility and gigantic status, it can be scary. The only way to survive the "newness" of it all would be to cling to the one that brought you there. It just makes sense!

Proverbs 3:5-6

Trust in the Lord with all your heart; don't rely on your own intelligence. Know him in all your paths, and he will keep your ways straight.

Let's break these verses down.

Verse 5, "Trust in the Lord with all your heart; don't rely on your own intelligence." Let us look at this verse in light of supply and demand. "Supply and demand are perhaps one of the most fundamental concepts of economics and it is the backbone of a market economy. Demand refers to how much (quantity) of a product or service is desired by buyers. The quantity demanded is the amount of a product people are willing to buy at a certain price; the relationship between price and quantity demanded is known as the demand relationship. Supply represents how much the market can offer. The quantity supplied refers to the amount of a certain good producers are willing to supply when receiving a certain price. The correlation between price and how much of a good or service is supplied to the market is known as the supply relationship. Price, therefore, reflects supply and demand." (Economic Basics: Supply and Demand) This verse speaks to the truth that the supply of God's help is totally contingent upon the hunger of the vessel. I am convinced that God does not move beyond two things: our ability to have faith in him and our willingness to sacrifice. Trust simply means to confide in. When you confide in something it literally means that you thrust all of yourself into it because you find safety as well as the necessary help needed in tough moments. This verse also gives us a demand to not lean on our own intellect. Our intellect without God is tied solely to this Cosmos which does not offer the necessary guidance in order to make God decisions. When we shun our intelligence, we open up to receive the supernatural intelligence of God our Father. Verse 6: "Know him in all your paths, and he will keep your ways straight." This verse points to the fact that we must know God. The only way to know God is to develop a relationship with Him. When we allow God into all of our plans, we set ourselves up for success. Proverbs 16:3, "Share your plans with the LORD, and you will succeed." God will collaborate with us through covenant and provide us with the wisdom, guidance, intelligence, clarity, and insight that is needed. Yes, He will be the God of providence in our lives. He will become the pathway needed for us to arrive at our desired place. God will keep us from walking in ignorance and folly. He will secure our ankles and cause our feet to be planted on the straight path and not the crooked path.

Prayer:

Father in Jesus' name, I honor you again. I appreciate you for the small places. At times, the small places seem like the cursed places. With little room to grow and limited resources, we can feel as if we have been given the weaker hand of life. However, Father, I thank you that you have blessed us to know through your spirit that the small places are the blessed places. It is in these places that like Amos, we too can come into another revelation of who we are and what we have to offer society. However, on one path, you will retract us back in order that we might regain a deeper focus of you and self. Though we weep much, groan much and experience great failure, we know that just like Amos we too will come out into a large place. A place of greater purpose expanded vision and a sharper perspective. Thank you for the small places. Thank you for being with us in these places. Thank you for causing us to be re-routed.

Chapter 3

A Stutter and A Word

God has a sense of humor. I went through some trauma and began to stutter. About eight years after the sudden onset of this stutter I found out that I was called to preach His Gospel. This really brought on a state of laughter and confusion for me. I felt like Moses:

Exodus 4:10

Moses raised another objection to God: "Master, please, I don't talk well. I've never been good with words, neither before nor after you spoke to me. I stutter and stammer."(MSG)

I had to go into my secret closet and talk to God about how I felt concerning his choice to use me in an area that I felt crippled in. I simply said, "Now Lord you know, see and hear my plight. How can I preach your Word when I have a hard time speaking?" The Lord simply said to me, "I will remove every flattering lip and every stuttering tongue." I again felt like Moses except this time I felt some relief:

Exodus 4:11-12

God said, "And who do you think made the human mouth? And who makes some mute, some deaf, some sighted, some blind? Isn't it I, God? So, get going. I'll be right there with you—with your mouth! I'll be right there to teach you what to say." (MSG)

This released great settlement into my heart. I thought, finally the Lord is going to instantaneously remove the thing that I believed could stop me from being a success at his Word spoken over my life. The stutter or stammer did not have the potency to stop the word of the Lord, only my thoughts about it did. Little did I know that it would be a journey to exercise my faith. I literally would have to depend on God to help me talk. Some people's miracle is that God delivered them from cigarettes, doubt, laziness, procrastination, etc. My greatest miracle was making it to the end of a sentence. I would practice preaching in my places of residence. I would pick a Scripture, do some study, grab a pencil and imagine that I was delivering God's Word to an audience. If I would stumble over a word I would stop, reflect and then try to choose a word similar to the word that I had trouble enunciating and keep on preaching. (ha.ha.ha...) Then God spoke to my heart and helped me to know that speaking is just a mind thing. You must hear yourself say it first in your mind and then say it with your mouth. If your mind isn't clear, then your words would not be clear. Having this perspective helped me tremendously. From the time that I would prepare privately to the time that I had to stand behind a podium to teach, preach or prophesy I would find that I needed the help of God. My greatest joy would be that after I sat down, I could reflect and see how the Lord miraculously caused my tongue to properly enunciate the words necessary to deliver the sermon.

However, I would like to take another perspective on this subject of a stutter. When we think of stutter, we normally think of flawed speech. According to Webster stutter can mean, to move or act in a halting or spasmodic manner. It could also mean to speak with involuntary disruption or blocking of speech. While delayed speech can be one facet of a stutter it is not the only facet. I want to talk about the involuntary disruptions that occur in our lives, which blocks the steady flow of our purpose. What I mean is that a stutter could also represent perversion, pornography, cheating on taxes, lying tongue, lewdness, debauchery, etc. What are those involuntary disruptions in your life that keep creeping up that you really do not want to entertain but you find yourself doing so anyway? The good that you would do you find yourself not doing. What is it? Can you identify these disruptions in your life and why is it? After you identify it take time out to ask the Lord to deliver you from them all.

Prayer:

Father God in the name of Jesus, you have a sense of humor. Yes, you make me laugh. You take pleasure in using the things that would seem most unusable to make the impossible, possible. Father, you have always taken pleasure in using foolish things to confound the wise. You have used liars, paupers, cheaters, religious people and now in the life of Moses, stutters to bring about your word in the earth. Thank you for choosing them and now God, thank you for using me as a part of your good plan. Father in the name of Jesus please help me with every involuntary disruption in my life that I seem to not have control over. Make my spirit ready to receive of your divine help. Thank you for the victory. In Jesus' mighty name.

Chapter 4

Involuntary Disruptions

Let's look at involuntary disruption from another viewpoint besides wrestling with a spirit of fornication, cheating, etc. Let's look at it from the viewpoint of going through warfare just to receive an answer from the Lord. All you did was pray and fast and look like all of hell broke loose against you. Let's look at it from that standpoint.

Daniel, called Belteshazzar had just come into a vision from the Lord which spoke of great war and hardship in the times to come. The prophet was moved to mourn and fast on behalf of this coming disaster. I believe that the Prophet believed that his prayers and sacrifices would in some way reach beyond heaven's borders and touch the heart of God. Doing this surely would cause what was to come to be turned around.

Daniel 10:1-3

In the third year of Cyrus king of Persia a thing was revealed unto Daniel, whose name was called Belteshazzar; and the thing was true, but the time appointed was long: and he understood the thing, and had understanding of the vision.

2 In those days I Daniel was mourning three full weeks.

3 I ate no pleasant bread, neither came flesh nor wine in my mouth, neither did I anoint myself at all, till three whole weeks were fulfilled. (KJV)

What amazed me while reading Daniel 10, was that the angel of the Lord visits the prophet to be of comfort to him through the confirmation that his prayers met the ear gates of heaven since the time he set his face to mourn, fast and pray. However, the prophet Daniel had come into great involuntary warfare with an evil Prince. This was an involuntary disruption in which Daniel had no control over.

Daniel 10:12

Then said he unto me, Fear not, Daniel: for from the first day that thou didst set thine heart to understand, and to chasten thyself before thy God, thy words were heard, and I am come for thy words. (KJV)

We can take a lesson from this mighty prophet, Daniel. Daniel was dedicated towards a cause and though he was dedicated he did not see any results. Though Daniel seemed barren in his pursuit he still pursued what he felt in his heart to do. Notice that his determination to start this spiritual journey was not about himself. His adamancy to continue his spiritual seeking journey was because he had a nation of people in view. In other words, his sacrifice was not selfish. Daniel did not quit or become sidetracked because he did not see the answers to his prayers in the time frame that he prayed for them to be answered. As a matter of fact, it was not until Daniel was through with his sacrifice of mourning, praying and fasting that he was visited by the angel of the Lord. This is encouraging because it speaks to the fact that sometimes we must remain faithful even though we seem forgotten or not heard by the Lord or by angels that assist us while in our heavenly pursuits.

Though Daniel had gained success by being heard, he became a target and threat to the Persian prince. When we are fought by principalities, spiritual wickedness, etc. in high places it is only because we have tapped into our purpose and have become effective in our approach. This angers the demonic world and causes there to be great attacks sent out to block the movement of fulfillment. I could only imagine that while Daniel was praying, the great amount of doubt that attacked his thoughts on whether or not the Lord heard his cry. Can you imagine going to the throne of grace day and night only to see nothing happen? Daniel did not see or hear anything at the time of his praying. Daniel may have felt rejected by God and felt that maybe he was not the right pick to intercede on behalf of any nation of people. Look at how the angel of the Lord had to make a special visit to the prophet to help him see something that he just could not see. The angel of the Lord had to help the Prophet's spiritual sight to see that he was in spiritual warfare with a principality. It was a principality which was later identified as the prince of Persia.

Daniel 10:13

"But the prince of the kingdom of Persia withstood me one and twenty days: but, lo, Michael, one of the chief princes, came to help me; and I remained there with the kings of Persia." (KJV)

This is a good place to pause and realize that though Daniel was a prophet and intercessor, he still could not see the very thing that was blocking his progress. Wait a minute. How could the praying prophet not see the root of this problem? It is my perspective that maybe God did not allow for the prophet to see the enemy because it would have shifted his focus off what he was supposed to do, which was to pray.

Let us pause right here and look a little deeper into this matter. There are some enemies that will be fighting us, and we can feel them fighting us, but God will not allow for us to see what it is or where it is. This can be a very frustrating place as I had experienced it many times. I would know that I was in warfare, but it did not matter how hard I would pray about it, I just would not see what "it" was. It would typically be in times where either I was fasting, praying or in a season where I had to make a God decision. What does this sound like to you? Yes, you got it, a season of divine assignment and divine focus. This prophet Daniel was under a mighty assignment from the Lord to pray on behalf of a nation. Had the Lord revealed who this enemy of his was he may have been discoursed from what really mattered. Are you saying that waring against this principality was not important? Not at all. However, what I am saying is that it was not Daniel's battle to fight. God already had an angel standing by to go to war on behalf of Daniel while he stayed focused on his assignment, which was to pray. You see my dear friends it is the devils' job to distract us from our first assignment which is to pray. He wants us to be so caught up in what's happening to us until we are blinded from seeing what is happening for us in the heavenlies. I want to encourage someone right here. Oh yes, I hear a song in my spirit right now:

Saints don't stop praying for the Lord is Nigh
Don't stop praying He'll hear your cry
For the Lord has promised and His word is true
Just don't stop praying
He'll answer you

I want to prophesy that your focal point is being strengthened and that the Lord is causing you to remain focused on what is most important. You will not be side tracked. You will be steadfast, immovable and always abiding in your assignment having the assurance and confidence that

God already has your help prepared. For this battle that you are in is not yours but it's the Lords. Now, come on clap your hands and sing along with me:

Saints don't stop praying for the Lord is Nigh
Don't stop praying He'll hear your cry
For the Lord has promised and His word is true
Just don't stop praying
He'll answer you

Yes beloved, God already had help (angels) that He would use to take care of this Persian demonic force. Prophets are natural warriors. If they see, sense or hear anything foreign then they would go after it. God possibly did not want Daniel to worry about defeating a devil that would eventually be defeated by another means. I believe it was Daniel's prayers that was the driving force or foundation of breakthrough. We can read that eventually the prince of Persia was defeated. Defeat of any spiritual force is a result of prayer. Prayer between a child of God and their Master (Jesus Christ) is communication that releases strength, strategy, peace, comfort and eventually defeat of the thing that would dare rise to defeat us. You see, while God is working out the details, He needs willing vessels that will not count it robbery to labor in prayer on any subject. I believe that while Daniel was praying there was some roaring going on in the heavenlies, it was Daniel's prayers that helped to get the job done.

I want to encourage someone in this moment that have been interceding for any length of time and the situation still seems barren or without results. You must know that just like Daniel, that though he was praying he did not see the root of the hold up. Daniel kept praying. God sent divine help to help him see the trouble. God also sent help to him to help him know that things were being worked out behind the scenes.

Daniel 10:13b

"but, lo, Michael, one of the chief princes, came to help me; and I remained there with the kings of Persia."

You see in this verse how Michael was being sent to help assist the angel deliver the message. We know Michael the Archangel is known as the warrior. In my understanding, Michael showed up to defeat the grips of this evil prince so that the message would be loosed. While Daniel was praying things were happening behind the scenes. God was defeating the delay. May the God of heaven send you divine help to defeat every delay in your life. May you be a constant in the Kingdom of our Lord and Savior Jesus Christ and one that is committed to prayer. May you be like Daniel and pray until you see something happen. Hold on dear brother. Be strong my dear sister. God is working on your behalf. Your answer is on the way! Keep praying. It was an evil spiritual entity that was standing in the way of the prayers that Daniel was sending up and the answers that God had sent through the angel. Now you have got to be thinking what I am thinking, and that is, this must have been a powerful wicked force in that it was able to delay the prayers of a seasoned prophet of God and an angel whose assignment was to break through barriers and deliver Kingdom messages. It did not matter how powerful this devil was. All we need to concern ourselves with is that Daniel won in the end.

Chapter 5

Voluntary Disruptions

We have examined what an involuntary disruption looks like through one of the daunting yet resolved trials of Daniel. We have seen that Daniel's situation was out of his control. However, I want to point out some voluntary disruptions of our purpose that we cause on ourselves. When something is voluntary, it simply means that it is willfully done. Voluntary means that one has chosen to take this route therefore in the end of any matter we have no one to fault but ourselves. Some of the willful atrocities experienced in this life include, but are not limited to, sexually perverted acts, procrastination, lying, unlawful drug use, rebellion, lasciviousness, un-forgiveness, etc. entertaining these spirits can and will lead one into spiritual diaspora. Yes, volunteering one's self to interact with any of these spirits will cause one to be castrated and scattered away from their purpose in this life.

Chapter 6

Keeping Up

We want nothing more than to keep up with the "Jones." Oh, come on. Don't you fight me on this line. You know that there has been a time or two where you found yourself feeling blue only because you didn't have what your close friend had. You were congratulating them on the job offer but you were saying how it would have been better had you got it. You told them to their face that their brand-new Porsche was such a blessing but inwardly you were thinking that you would look better in it. Oh, come on here church and be honest. Lol!!!! People define success by whatever it is that they hold as valuable. Considering career, some people think that being a Lawyer, Doctor, CEO of a Fortune 500 company, etc. as being a success. Others may deem being an EMS, Nurse, construction worker, port Worker, etc. as being a success. As it concerns relationship stats, some people deem being married with 5 children a success. Others may deem being married with no children a success. As it relates to living status, some people view living in a

$1.5-million-dollar home as successful living. Others may feel that a $175,000 3-bedroom 2.5 bath home is success. I have learned that success is whatever one holds as being valuable. I have had hundreds of conversations with people about their current life satisfactions and to my surprise, 65% of the conversants were disappointed with the status of their lives. Most of these people in my eyes were doing quite well. However, the more I began to talk with these people I then realized that 75% of the reason why most of them were unhappy was because they were comparing their lives with the lives of their contemporaries. I was reminded of the Scripture through the penmanship of the Apostle Paul found in *2 Corinthians 10:12:*

"For we do not make bold to rank or to compare ourselves with certain of those commending themselves, but they, among themselves measuring themselves, and comparing themselves with themselves, are not wise," (YLT)

Some of the People that I had conversations with and were unhappy were college students with a bright future, Business owners, Sheriffs of high rank, Medical personnel, ministers of the Gospel, etc. These people in my eyes were a success. They were loved and liked by the people that they served, their family members, and spoken highly of. I then realized that when one does not like himself or herself, they have the tendency to magnify what is "lacking" in their lives as measured against their success perspectives thus abandoning what God and others see as great and useable. In every one of these people, I saw greatness and high potential. It was just sad to see how what I saw and what they saw did not comply. This attitude impeded them from inspiring others. We fail to realize that when God made us, He made us good. He made us to be unique not having to feel as if we had to keep up with anyone or anything except His Words spoken into us. Let us examine:

Genesis 1:31:

"God saw all that he had made, and it was very good. And there was evening, and there was morning--the sixth day."(NIT)

God has made all things for His good pleasure according to:

Colossians 1:16:

"For in him all things were created: things in heaven and on earth, visible and invisible, whether thrones or powers or rulers or authorities; all things have been created through him and for him." (NIT)

Genesis 1:31 helps us to know that on the sixth day God made a public announcement that what was made was "good" in His eyes. He was pleased with what he saw. Apart of this creation pleasure was you and me. So, this means that God liked the way we were and our genetic make-up. This means that before we ever built anything, went to school, decided on what our living conditions would be (house, apartment, trailer, RV) etc., decided on a spouse, what our financial statuses would be, etc., God liked us. This is great news because it shows that God's attraction towards us was never based upon anything that we accumulated in this life but solely upon how He had made us from the beginning. God chose the book of Genesis, or the book of beginning, to establish this concept with mankind. I believe that this was because God knew the pressures and competitions that would soon arise with mankind. He knew that man would later try to establish what status of life one would need to have in order to be deemed as being blessed by God or even that God was with him. Therefore Jesus had to establish this biblical and very relevant truth with His disciples found in Luke 12:15:

"And he said unto them, Take heed, and beware of covetousness: for a man's life consisteth not in the abundance of the things which he possesseth."(KJB)

Jesus wanted his disciples to know that a true sign that God was with them was not tied to how much money they had, the size of their home, the brand of their car, how fancy their clothes were or anything of the natural. However, the sign that God was with you was simply that He had a hand in your development and that His hands were on your life throughout the course of your life. In Colossians 1:16 Paul lets us know that we were made for Him. This means that the greatest purpose that man was made was to be an open vessel used in whatever capacity needed in the Lord's kingdom. When we yield ourselves over to the Lord for the purposes of promoting His agenda, we are guaranteed His approval and his help.

We become blinded by God's approval of us when we allow the spirit of competition to arise. We lose focus on what God requires of us and start to put great attention upon what we think would make us accepted by man. You would be surprised to know that the agenda for many that produce a book, business, etc. do so out of a spirit of competition. It's not necessarily that they heard God to do so because of a need for it in the earth, but more so to Keep up with their friends, relatives or co-workers. It's ridiculous.

Ephesians 1:6

"To the praise of the glory of his grace, wherein he hath made us accepted in the beloved."

We are already accepted by God and do not need to do anything special to be accepted by man. The Scripture teaches us that it is God that will give us favor with God and man. This means that it is not our job to seek who we should be favored by. God knows all things. He knows who we need to be connected to in every season of our lives. It is because we desire to be successful in the eyes of our contemporaries that we would despise anyone or anything that would dare stand in our way of achieving "our" goals.

Prayer:

Father in the name of Jesus it is because of your mercies that I am not consumed. So, I say great are your mercies towards me. Father, I thank you for your truth that is revealed to me through your word. Your word declares that we have a place in you and that if we are willing and obedient, we will have the good of the land. This was a promise in biblical days, and it is still a promise today. For you are the same today, yesterday and forever more. Father, I thank you that you make me sure of your promises and that I do not have a need to compete with anyone in order to receive from you the promises of your word. For I am confident that my promises are secure with you. Yes Father, I thank you that every promise of God is yea and amen. Therefore, I will wait on you. I thank you that the spirit of competition is not a part of my DNA. Whatever I do is only because you have instructed me to do so. I thank you father that there is no need in me to produce for the sake of a show. Father as I wait, I only ask that you give me the strength and encouragement in my very soul. Yes, as you process me and prepare me, help me to occupy until the appointed time. Amen.

Chapter 7

Wait

While looking through Liberty universities' hiring page I stumbled across the question and answer post page. The question posted was, "How long does it take to get hired from start to finish? What are the steps along the way?" As I scrolled down, I saw that there were three replies. The former Resident Admissions Counselor said it took two weeks. The former Athletic Facilities Assistant said that it could take one week. However, when I got to the last response it posted, "It takes about 6 months to be hired. The process is rigorous. You must be a Godly person." This statement had been posted by a current Online Adjunct Professor, Dissertation Chairperson. I am not sure if you caught what I did. I noticed that the first two replies were posted by two former Liberty University employees whose process to be hired was shorter than the current Liberty University employee, whose process to be hired was longer. Liberty University is a fine Christian institution that was established by the late Jerry Falwell. This Christian institution has been a blessing to its city by creating hundreds of jobs for people looking for the opportunity to grow and work in a Christian atmosphere. The university has even created jobs for students that were looking for ways to earn a good and free education from a fully accredited college. Being selected to work in any capacity at Liberty University is a huge deal. To be selected to become a staff member meant some good cash, good relationships, positive environment, job opportunities and a free education. What more could you ask for?

While having all the good qualities of such prestigious opportunity one would need to consider the process that it would take to be fully equipped. To have longevity while working with such a company will take time and effort. Who is to say that the former employees did not have some legit reason for not staying long with the institution? However, I do know that longevity on any job is highly linked to a long process of having to wait to be employed due to weeks of training, probationary periods, tedious interviews, background checks, etc. The longer the seeking employee had to wait puts more value on the position that they would hold.

This waiting period really blessed me in that I was able to see that the one who had to wait the longest and go through the greatest process is the one that is still standing with the vision of the university today. I can only imagine that what is helping to keep this person faithful to this position is the fact that they remember the process. Yes, what it took for them to be hired for the job. Being questioned before those with doctorates, being critiqued without knowing whether or not they would be picked, risking time, energy and efforts. I'm sure all of this has really helped this individual to remain fruitful in the position that he is in today. I want to flip this around with the waiting process in the spiritual aspect. How long have you had to wait to be where you are today in the kingdom of the Lord? How tedious has the process been for you? Why did you stick with the process? I want to encourage you that it may have seemed like you've been in a long waiting period. It may seem as if your preparation process is beyond what you anticipated. Yes, I can identify with you. You feel like throwing up your hands and pursuing the life that you want to live. You may even be questioning whether or not you are on the right track. Granted, you feel as if you should have seen a harvest of fruit by now. I want you to be encouraged to know that the harvest is not your responsibility. Yes beloved, how much fruit you produce or when you produce is God's responsibility. Your only job is to be obedient to every command of the Lord.

Let's look quickly at the story of Hannah. Hannah was one of the wives of Elkanah. She was loved by Elkanah but she had a problem. Hannah's problem was that she was loved but she was also barren. In the biblical days, if a man's wife could not produce him a man child, she would be despised and looked down upon. Elkanah had another wife by the name of Peninnah. Peninnah was the wife that produced Elkanah children at first. It would seem as though Peninnah should show Hannah some encouragement but instead she used it as an opportunity to taunt her.

1 Samuel 1:7

Year after year it was the same—Peninnah would taunt Hannah as they went to the Tabernacle. Each time, Hannah would be reduced to tears and would not even eat.

Let's stop right here for a moment. Some of you are in a situation where instead of you being encouraged through your season of despair you are being harassed. I want you to remember that this is how the enemy operates. He investigates our lives to see what ails our very soul. He does this in order that he might become a thorn in our side over it. The portion of Hannah's story that baffled me was the fact that though she was a praying woman and dedicated to the temple, she was still bothered by this Peninnah. This shows that though we are committed to prayer there are some things that can still bother our souls. What I am saying is that you are human, and humans feel. Say amen church. However, something happened with Hannah. She developed a non-tolerance for spiritual harassment.

1 Samuel 1:9-11

⁹ Once after a sacrificial meal at Shiloh, Hannah got up and went to pray. Eli the priest was sitting at his customary place beside the entrance of the Tabernacle. [10] Hannah was in deep anguish, crying bitterly as she prayed to the Lord. [11] And she made this vow: "O Lord of Heaven's Armies, if you will look upon my sorrow and answer my prayer and give me a son, then I will give him back to you. He will be yours for his entire lifetime, and as a sign that he has been dedicated to the Lord, his hair will never be cut.

Hannah got up and went to pray but this time her prayers were different. Precious people, you got to realize that if you have been praying a certain way for some time and nothing has changed, and your enemy still has access to your emotions then this is a sign that you have got to shift the way you are praying and what you are praying. Hannah got fed up with that taunting demon in Peninnah and took her anguish and bitterness to the temple. She laid on that altar and prayed out of her soul. This time Hannah was not praying for God to bless her just so that she could prove to Peninnah that God was with her womb as well. This time she made a vow to the Lord that if he blessed her, the child would be a kingdom blessing. I believe that this was what God was waiting to hear come out of Hannah's prayers. God had a set time for when Hannah should bring forth a child. Hannah just had to realize it and accept the fact that God would do it but in his timing. All God wanted her to do was to keep waiting and wailing. Somebody has got to understand that what's in you will come forth at just the right time. Both Samuel's conception and birth were prophetic. He was not an ordinary child. He was born to change the trajectory of the whole prophetic movement. This child Samuel that Hannah had was so significant that no word he spoke would hit the ground. In other words, everything he said would be in direct alignment with God's plans for that time and thus he would always have the support of heaven. You do not see anything in the bible about Pennianh's children yet 2 books in the bible is dedicated to Hannah's child Samuel. Hannah had to endure hardship by waiting a while. Yes, she was getting older. Yes, people were mocking her. Yes, she was fed up and so was her husband. However, her dedication to the waiting process had eventually removed the reproach from her.

While you wait it does not mean that your emotions will not be attacked. I am here to tell you that they will be attacked. For those of you that have been burdened by the Lord to preach on faith and blessings prepare to be challenged to see others blessed while you wait on your own fulfillment. However, I want to encourage you that in just a little while longer you are going to see the benefits of what you have been wailing, weeping, praying and fasting for. Hold on. Your answer is just about to land. It's ok to be angry. Just don't sin. Its ok to express the true sentiments of how you feel about your situation to God. He can handle it. It's ok to be a cry baby in the presence of the Lord. He won't judge you. This is the one place where you can relinquish all your ego, power and authority and God will not take it as an advantage to bruise you or use it against you. He will not demote you. He is not like man. Be like Hannah and take it to a safe place. God will give you the strength to get up again, to wait another day. So, I leave this section with this, weep, roll, pout, cry, etc... But please beloved do me and you a favor and DO NOT QUIT! Selah

Prayer:

Father in the name of Jesus, I thank you once again. God this place called waiting is such a trying yet rewarding place for those that will keep going. Many are weary. Many are discouraged. Father, I thank you that you are sending a fresh wind into their lives. Father you are rejuvenating their weak bones and placing a new mantle of supernatural strength upon them right now. I thank you father that like Hannah you are causing them to know that their waiting periods are not rejection from you, but it's only a sign that you are preparing something far and exceedingly greater than what they could ever think. Yes, Lord I thank you that your word encourages us that you will do exceedingly and abundantly and that you will go beyond what we have ever thought of. Father restore the hope of your people. Pastor it's not over for your ministry. Prophet you will make it. Apostle you will get through this. Wait I say on the Lord and be of good cheer. God will strengthen your heart. Oh, yes, He's doing it right now. Allow your faith to connect with your help. Amen.

Chapter 8

Season of Weeping

Ecclesiastes 3:4

"a time to weep and a time to laugh..."

Weeping. Where do I begin? Everyone weeps. People weep over a lost loved one. People weep over disappointments. People weep over being unemployed. People weep because their feelings are hurt. People weep over receiving bad news. But there is also joyful weeping such as weeping over a child graduating from college, a daughter or son getting married, a daughter having her first child, a son having his first child. The joys of life can bring on tears. However, the kind of weeping that Solomon was writing about in this third chapter of Ecclesiastes was not that of joy but that of pain and grief. According to Ellicott's Commentary for English Readers, this word weeping was referring to noisy funeral lamentations. After reading this observation I quickly understood that it was weeping over situations that did not seem favorable or satisfying to the weeper. I was quickly able to identify with the writer. Having gone through some very disappointing and difficult situations, weeping became my only resort. I remember going to a church service that I was late attending. I quietly stepped in and a Prophet had called me out and asked me to come to the front. I was perplexed because I wasn't coming to service looking for any prophecy let alone to be asked to come to the front of the church. Some of what this preacher had said was simply, "you've been suffering and suffering for a long time. God says if you give him a yes, the next 6 months of your life are getting ready to change." Wow. This was shocking because most words that I received were words of a great future. Words such as preaching before the masses, being greatly anointed, living large, being on television, etc... All to which I believe is true because it was only confirmations of what God had shared with me privately. However, I was humbled to have someone tap into my "current situation." While I appreciated and respected all who had previously spoken into my life, I was most appreciative that this prophet whom I did not know called out the painful circumstance in which I was faced with at the time. You see preaching, I did it. Ministering in song, I did it. Leading praise and worship wherever I was planted, I did it. Working with the youth, I did it. Working with the women's department, I did it, leading intercessory prayer in ministries, I did it. Accepting ministry engagements outside of my home church, I did it. I was committed to being a ministry gift to ministries but not so much of being a gift to myself. I felt like my life was mundane. I felt like the children of Israel going around the mountain forever and not really seeing results in my personal life. Anointed I am. I say this with all humility and that I know that God's hand is upon my life. Wherever I would go and whatever service that I would be a part of, God would be with me through the undeniable evidence of His anointing. However, in my personal life it seemed very hard to succeed. You may ask the question, "How is it that you are anointed and had such a difficult time in your personal life?" Doesn't the anointing destroy yokes? These were my exact sentiments. I was so faithful that I was given a trophy and award from my leaders at the time, which stated- Most Consistent Growth. I still have that trophy today. I was dedicated not for man's sake but because I really loved God and just wanted to be a ministry gift. I thought because I was going to school and being faithful to promote the kingdom of God that all of what concerned me was to fall into place. Well, didn't you go to school to receive an education? Yes, I did but after having tried to pass what should have been a simple test, I failed. I did not fail 1 time I failed 7 times. I would go to tutoring sessions but still, fail. I got tired of failing and began a journey towards something else that I thought would benefit me financially as well as helping me to stay active in church. Those test failures were always failings of only a few points. I would go back, study, and then try again and the same results would occur. When you failed a test, it would reveal the area, which you were short of knowledge. I would study in that area and still fail. Only this time the failure was in another area. It was crazy. I started thinking that there was a hitman. Lol! I thought that someone was intentionally making me fail. Surely there was someone at the head department failing me. Lol! I just did not understand. I started to feel despondent. I started to feel as if maybe I should not be as optimistically thoughtful for myself. I thought that maybe I was aiming too high. Maybe I was not to ever try school. Let's pause here. This was my mindset though I kept being faithful at achieving my goals. The devil was blinding me. I had a 3.05 GPA and was passing all of my classes with A's and B's and was still moving forward. However, I began to dismiss all this success and magnify what was lacking. This is how the enemy works. He will blind you from what is working in your life and blow up before you what is not seemingly working in your life. However, you have got to keep pressing on. When the devil throws stuff up in your face, remind him of all of the other accomplishments that God has helped you with. Don't let the devil make you feel low. God has raised you up and has made you to be seated in heavenly places. This was a testing and development of my faith walk with God. Failure was not an option, so I kept on going.

However, while I kept going, I still had a war going on in my mind, "Oh Lord," I thought, "I have wasted my time, efforts and energy." I finally graduated. God is good. After one triumph came another mountain. Lord have mercy. I got frustrated because after receiving my degree I was unable to find employment that would be accommodating. While we celebrate a victory, we cannot rest in it. We have got to keep our spiritual antennas up because that devil is forever looking for ways to hit us. Though I was employed, it was not at the salary that I had in mind. I still had to thank God for it. However, it got so bad that I used to hate offering time sometimes. Lol. When you've been in church as long as I have you would understand that most times the preachers would tell you what to give. I would come to church praising God that I even had $25.00 to sow. I would arrive only to find out that at the end of the sermon you would be asked to sow $125.00 based on Mark 12 and verse 5, (which was the text that was taken to preach from.) lol. Even though the bible says to give cheerfully and with the measure that you have been given, many people don't. To be honest some people stand up with their offering ostentatiously to send a message across the room that they are not struggling financially. The motives are impure. When you are a leader and people know that you are a leader, if no one stands up to sow the seed that is asked for the leaders are expected to stand up with it and with a smile on their faces. Please do not take this the wrong way.

I like to give. Yes, sometimes my giving would be a sacrifice. However, if the Lord has specifically told you what to give in a service then you should not try to impress people by giving beyond what you know God told you. You absolutely cannot beat God's giving no matter how hard you try. However, there are times when God will say sow $50.00 but the preacher is asking for $95.00. Sometimes the preacher will ask for a $30.00 seed but you may hear God say sow $230.00. Your blessing is in sowing whatever you hear God say to give. You just have to trust God with your seeds.

Back to the weeping portion…My journey has been long and seemingly repetitive. Going through a battle in my mind, emotions, finances and even some church confusion is all a part of the processing of God. When you are prophesied over, all of hell breaks out against you. Its intent is to make you feel so inadequate that you would just lose hope in that God would help you through your processing. The Word of God shows us that hope deferred makes the heart sick. If the devil can get you to become hopeless then he would win.

I spent many years in a university trying to figure out what I wanted to be and do with my life. I am not one to easily give up. Yes, I am a prophet of God but sometimes when we hear we hear only in part.

1 Corinthians 13:9,

"For we know in part, and we prophesy in part."

I would set out on a route and then after some time of not seeing any results I would rethink on whether or not I was on the right track. I know what you might be saying, " Ashley, you have to stick with something for the long run and not give up so quickly." I hear you, but, baby 5 years is no short time. Lol! You must admit that if you are doing something for some time and not seeing any manifestation, you would have to try another path. Insanity is doing something over and over and expecting a different result. I tried other paths for the same degree and that did not work. So I got it. I simply thought, "Ok God, I get it." Yes, I went to school and have received degrees but there was always a void inside. I never wanted to be poor or without. When I was in elementary school I always said to myself that I would go to school and be sufficient. Doing this would ensure that I would not have to ask others for their financial help if needed. My point is that I have always wanted to be self-sufficient. My mother and father both did well. My mother went to nursing school and became a top nurse in her class. My dad went to the police academy and became a well-respected police officer. I wanted to be like my parents and be a well-respected citizen who earned her money rightly. I do not like asking others for help unless I could not help myself. Some say that this is pride, but I saw it as being responsible and not a burden on anyone else. I would always try to present myself better than what I was going through. Though I was feeling inward lack, at least when I looked in the mirror I didn't look like it. There is a song that was written by Deon Kipping, "I Don't look Like What I've Been Through." At least this was my testimony.

I had a degree, student loans and no "real" job to cover the monthly payments. I felt so silly. I laughed at myself and said girl what have you gotten yourself into? Remind you that though I got an education degree I got it the non-certified way. This meant that the only job that I could get as an educator would be as a teacher assistant or a substitute teacher. This would only ensure between $300-450 a week. Let us be real that after paying bills with both checks a month there would not be anything left to spend. Lol. I finally yelled at God, "It's a curse. Right God. I'm cursed." I mean after putting in at other jobs that my degrees could have possibly worked and being rejected, I felt cursed. The Lord then took me to

Lamentations 3:37

"Who can command things to happen without the Lord's permission?" (NIV)

God spoke to me and said, "It's your process." Say what Lord? "What do you mean by a process?" I thought I just went through a process? What does being processed mean? Perform a series of mechanical or chemical operations on (something) in order to change or preserve it. When the army processes you during recruitment, you enter a long-haired civilian and come out a shaven headed soldier (vocabulary.com). God was helping me to know that my degrees were not my source but that He would be my source. I would have to trust his guidance. He helped me to know that I had pride in me that He wanted to strip out of me. That attitude that is too full of pride to ask for help. You see, God was letting me know that I was literally going through a stripping. Take the s off of stripping and you have tripping. So, in other words, he was also saying Ashley, you can stop tripping. Going through a process is not a fun period in life. It is a season of weeping, truth about who you really are, and refining, reshaping, etc. Going through this is not easy neither does it feel good. So, eventually one will start tripping. I mean I started giving God ultimatums like, "God if you don't hurry up, I'm quitting." "God if you don't move for me, I am going to go do what I want to do." Even though I would say these things I really didn't mean it because I have always had a fear that the day I stepped out of God's will that I would fall dead in that very hour. Lol. I would trip but still be moving forward with God in this long and mundane process. Though I would be mad, disappointed, angry, sad etc. I would still be found in the house of the Lord preaching, praising and giving God some worship. I must admit that these things have helped me in this long process. Dedication to the things of God while being processed is the birthing grounds for strength.

When something is processed it is taken through a series of stages towards perfection. It goes in as one thing and comes out another. When being processed with God, he picks the weak, lowly, rejected, etc. and takes them through a process and they come out strong, lifted, and knowing that they are accepted. One mentor shared with me that the longer God spends on you the longer you will last in His Kingdom. You see there are a number of things that God will come after while in the process; things like perversion of any type. I don't know about you, but I have counted more sexual perverted cases than any other type of cases within the church arena. Maybe these people had not allowed God to thresh it out of their souls completely before embarking upon their journeys in the Kingdom. Nonetheless it is one of the biggest pitfalls for many in the Lord's church. This, in my opinion, is a direct result of people that are depending on there degrees, talents and gifts to get them through instead of depending on God and the help of the Holy Spirit.

Jude 24

"Now all glory to God, who is able to keep you from falling away and will bring you with great joy into his glorious presence without a single fault."

This scripture really speaks to the truth that God is a keeper to all who desires to be kept by Him. Some other soul threshing that God does with those in the process is to thresh out lying, manipulation to get ahead in life, jealousy, envy, hatred, prejudice, un-forgiveness, etc. All these sins if not dealt with in our dark season can potentially cause great destruction not only to our lives but to the lives of those that would take an interest in our ministries. God helped me to know that obtaining my degree was good. However, he did not want me to give glory to my degrees but that in all things to give thanks and glory to him. I have now learned that the bible is right when it says that the righteous is never forsaken neither is his seed begging bread. I have made it my priority to live for God to the best of my ability. In return, God has taught me how to live by faith and to trust his plan. I have never gone without. I will not lie and say that at times I have not had to sacrifice one thing for another, but God has been good to me and I am thankful for the season of weeping and stripping. Though he is still stripping me. I can go through it with a greater confidence knowing that somehow and in the timing of the Lord shall I come forth as pure gold. However, in the words of Apostolic Bishop Roberts, "Despite what life brings, in every season one must still produce." Weep baby! Weep, but remain faithful. God will bring you through every time.

Prayer:

Father in the name of Jesus, I want to thank you for my season of weeping. Father I thank you that when I thought that I was ready to rise to success, how you pulled me back to strip me of things that could potentially damage my rise. Father yes it can be difficult to sit in a seat of weeping and have the ugly things in me come forth. To face me is not easy. However, I thank you that it is because of this phase of my life that I can truly focus on what is important in this life. I thank you that you have given me a new perspective and a new attitude about my life and journey with you. I thank you that for every other season of weeping that you will remind me that it's only for my good and that in the end, I will rise to higher heights not worrying about anything rising to demote me. In Jesus' name. Amen.

Chapter 9

No Wasted Time

We can all look back over our lives and see how we have wasted valuable and precious time. Sometimes we can embark on a journey that is mere wishful and selfish ambition. We at times get distracted and forget that God only expects us to do the portion that He has entrusted for us to do. Anything outside of His will for our lives is not necessary.

Proverbs 19:21

"Many are the plans in the mind of a man, but it is the purpose of the LORD that will stand." (ESV)

Can you think back to a time when you started doing things just because you saw your brother, sister or friend do it? You saw your friend who went to school for Community Development launch a Non-profit organization. All of a sudden you found yourself attempting the same project or one similar to your friends. However, though your friend's organization has lasted 7 plus years you found yourself burning out only after 6 months. This could be that you were trying to do something that you were not created to do.

Ecclesiastes 3:1

"For everything there is a season, a time for every activity under heaven." (NLT)

Another perspective to take is that you were striving to do something that you are called to do but out of season. We have a job to do and that is to ask God to identify what season we are in. The second thing that we must do once our season has been identified is to ask God to help us know both the timing and the activities that we must be doing while in that season. God will talk to you about something that you are not in the timing to do just yet. However, I submit to you that in every season there is something that God requires from us and heaven is ready to support. However, the key to receiving heaven's support is to be able to pinpoint what activity you are supposed to be doing. It's like a pregnant woman living through a 9-month waiting period. In every trimester something is supposed to happen. It's like her body is on this inevitable timetable. It does not matter how uncomfortable she is with carrying that baby inside of her, her body will not release a fully developed baby in month number 5. This is because of three things; she is still in the season of carrying and not birthing, her body's timing is off and what is inside of her is not fully developed. I submit to you my dear brothers and sisters that God grants us all a season of human growth development. That's right! God knows what we should look like after maturation. However, our maturation process can be ugly because we are still being formed into the way God wants us to be. The passageway to get there is not a pretty route. When we are brought forth too soon, we become more susceptible to disease which can cause our lifespan expectancy to be shorter.

Let's look at it from the creation of the earth. In the very beginning, God hid the earth under a massive amount of water. The earth was revealed to us in the beginning as without form, and void, and darkness. That is a rather useless state to be in only because it was in no shape to be useful for anyone. This could be the very reason that God did not bring any human on the planet earth until it passed through maturation. Anyway, even though the earth was without form and void, and darkness, God still had an awesome plan for it. Just like that growing baby in its mother's womb and like the underdeveloped earth, God will also provide dark and hidden places for us so that we could grow and when we come forth, we would be someone's hope. Notice how the earth did not come forth until God was ready to work on it. Even when the season came for God to work on it, he still worked on it in private. I believe that the purpose of this seclusion is to provide a safe place to grow without fail. Yes, God will provide safe and secluded places for us to properly develop. If God were to allow us to move forward with doing something that we were indeed called to do out of season, then we could easily fall prey to being spiritually diseased, thus dying spiritually. We would be more open to entertaining spirits of jealousy, pride, envy, perversion, lust, covetousness, etc.; all of which can lead to spiritual dis-ease. This would happen because we are not fully developed; therefore spiritual mentors, instructors and coaches are needed. They are to walk alongside you to help you in your discernment concerning the phase you are in with your development. You need someone to encourage you with knowing that you are an evangelist, teacher, pastor or prophet just as much as you need someone to tell you wait on your ministry. You need a corrected voice in your life in the flesh to tell you to sit down, to get rid of your lying spirit, to rid that lustful spirit, to get delivered from homosexuality, etc... before you step out into the public eye. No mercy is found in the public eye. You need someone to check your spirit before you go out there in the name of "Jesus" and in representation of your pastor. Say amen church.

Another wasted time of our lives is when we start doing things out of competition. Are we doing it because it's our time or because we don't want to feel left out or seem behind schedule.

Galatians 6:4

"Each one should test their own actions. Then they can take pride in themselves alone, without comparing themselves to someone else." (NIV)

The spirit of competition is dangerous and will have you on a long and fruitless path. I have never been a person of competition. I am not the one to look at the work of another and try to copy it. It has always been my spirit to celebrate or to encourage the works of another. I remember while pursuing a project single in my early twenties, one of the people that was assisting me tried to make me feel as if I had to beat another sister at completing her single. The person, let's just use the name Baker, said to me, "Hey Ash, come on now you've got to hurry up because Judy is almost done with her CD." I laughed and made no comment. When I was driving home, I thought about the whole conversation and realized that the individual was trying to make me feel as though I was in a competition with my dear sister. I was quickly given the help of the Lord to shake that foolishness out of my head. I refused to allow the enemy to use me by competing with my sister in the Lord. "The race is not given to the swift or the battle to the strong but to those that endure until the end." I prayed for my sister and asked that God would cause her single to be a success and that God would one day bless my endeavors as well. When I saw her, I made sure that I embraced her in front of the very ones who wanted to see division between us. I learned to defeat the assignment of the devil by doing what he did not want to see me do, which was to be loving, kind and genuine. I refused to waste my time being used by the devil. Let us look at one of many biblical stories whose root was jealousy and that resulted in competition.

Genesis 30:1

When Rachel saw that she was not bearing Jacob any children, she became jealous of her sister. So she said to Jacob, "Give me children, or I'll die! (NIV)

This battle between two sisters had gotten out of hand. Before Jacobs arrival to their land and to their father Laban's house, we do not hear of any rival. Both Leah and Rachel were faithful servants in the house of their father Laban. Leah was the oldest and Rachel was the youngest. Leah was described as the ugly duckling while Rachel was deemed to be very beautiful and shapely. Leah did not have a problem with Rachel's beauty or her not being married as long as no one affirmed the beauty of Rachel or wanted to marry her. I would like to take this moment to help someone know that there are some people that recognize your attractiveness in the kingdom. However, though they may have a problem with you being gifted they will probably never show it until you are requested for another level of service. Some people don't mind you being prophesied to just as long as you don't allow for circumstances wherein you can grow in that spoken word.

Genesis 30: 22-23

[22]Then God remembered Rachel; he listened to her and enabled her to conceive.23 She became pregnant and gave birth to a son and said, "God has taken away my disgrace." 24 She named him Joseph, and said, "May the Lord add to me another son. (NIV)

Rachel did not need to waste time quarreling with Leah because her time was coming to be fruitful. God did not forget her. God was just waiting on the right season to bring her into her fulfillment. I want to help someone to know that God has not forgotten about you. He is getting you ready so that when the season shows up, you can step into it.

Prayer:

Father, I thank you for allowing my eyes to be open to the fact that I have no time to waste. Father, I thank you that you cause me to produce when you are ready. I thank you that like Rachel, I too can stand still to see the salvation of the Lord. At times we are pressured by the status quos to hurry up and to be like others. At times we are challenged to step out before our time. Therefore, we waste time that could be used preparing to do things that we should not in the moment. Father help us to have strong discernment. Yes, Lord help us to be graced as the tribe of Issachar who could discern the times and the seasons. Father I also ask that you won't let me sit too long either, but father when my spirit receives the charge to move ahead that I will get up in full obedience and with strong faith knowing that you will help me to produce. I thank you father in Jesus' name. Amen.

Chapter 10

Relationship Harmony

I have made the mistake of trying to put all of my eggs into one basket. What I mean is that at one time in my life I had brought people who were meant to be my connection into most of my other connections. This was not a good idea. I learned a huge lesson. People who are assigned to you are not always purposed to relate to all of your other connections. You see some people don't really have your best interest at heart. People get jealous, envious and just vicious when they have inner issues. The Bible is right, misery loves company. Instead of people wanting to see your relationships blossom they plot to kill your positive connection. Now the genuine connections that God had given you are damaged. This leaves you open, vulnerable and now skeptical of who you can trust with the issues of your inner being. People are fickle. They sing your praises today and by tomorrow they are ready to destroy you. People will hate you on a buddy pass. They will allow the ill perception of another to control how they view you as a person. You will experience people who love being insubordinate towards you but when you return the same behavior, they will find it to be rude and disrespectful.

I had an incident on a job. There was this person who was considered a top employee. This person had been working for this company for a very long time. When I came along, they had sought to connect with me but there was something in my spirit that just would not agree with theirs. I started to develop good relationships with the other persons on the job and all of a sudden, this person went from being nice to talking to me in a really nasty way. The first couple of times that this person was unethical towards me, I let it go. I thought that maybe they were going through some hard situations and was just irate. This person had confided in me that their home life was in disarray. I prayed for them. I would try to build them up. It seemed like the nicer I got the nastier they became. I started to get agitated. Instead of me approaching them I told a supervisor. The supervisor sat me down in a room separated from anyone and admitted that other people had made complaints against this same irate person. However, he went on to say that he did not think that they meant to be so rude towards me. You should have seen the look on my face. Like really sir!!!! I mean, if others have made negative comments against them then Sir there is a problem. He went on to say that if they ever did it again then to notify him and he would have a talk with them. As time went on, they did calm down a little. However once again when they saw that I would talk to another employee and we would have a great time talking with one another, they became irate again. Well, one day I spoke up to this person and set them straight. They did not like it. They would influence the others by saying things against my character to them and after a while, they too started acting funny. I laughed and said Lord what is this. This person was just jealous.

I found out that this person wanted me to bring them into my inner circle. I tested them with a few of my connections and found out why I did not agree with their spirit in the beginning. I was not bothered by them spreading rumors about me but rather a little concerned that the few that I introduced them to would believe such foolishness. However, God told me not to hate them for it, but rather to see it through the eyes of God. When people secretly desire something you have, they will begin to operate by stealth. They will pretend that they are your friend when all they want is for you to bring them into every aspect of your life so that they can have access. This is dangerous. When that spirit in them sees that you are weak and down, that is when it will attack. However, be encouraged God will show you their hidden plans. God reveals what is hidden to those that pray. Beloved whatever the Lord reveals, do yourself a favor and believe him. The scripture reveals that everything that is done in the dark has its appointed time of being revealed. Nothing can remain hidden. People will hate that your pastor calls your name all the time. They will hate you because you are gifted. People will hate you because you can exegete or eisegesis the word of God well. People will hate you because you can minister in song. People will hate you because your boss likes you, you have long hair, you are tall, or that you have genuine relationships.

I want to help someone be reminded that you really can relax. You can be at ease. The people that your enemies have tried hard to damage your name and character before, and it worked, were not the people that you needed in your life. I learned quickly to let them have the ones that they discipled unto themselves. My eyes were opened to know that those were not really a divine connection in the beginning. I call them reeds shaken in the wind. I do not run after them. If they go, they just go. How ignorant of us to think that we need people who have chosen to believe a lie concerning who we are. It reveals what was already in their speculations of you in the beginning. You have so much to offer. You have a whole world of people that are waiting on you to minister to them and win them over. Everybody is not after you to kill you. Don't allow the enemy to make you feel that everybody is out to destroy you because that is a lie. God has genuine people for you. Trust him. When you find yourself being attacked by jealous people just pray and ask God to give you an outlet and I can assure you that He will. I want to encourage you that God will give you people that will move to the same drumbeat. You will have the same rhythm in the spirit and God will bless your union. What God puts together no man will be able to put asunder. Can 3 cords be easily broken? Not when God has done it. Let God choose your connections. Let him choose your friendships.

Prayer:

Father the race is not given to the swift nor to the strong but to those that would endure until the end. So, father I thank you that the end has come for me being tolerant of fake people. I thank you for the strength to let go of everything that has developed a problem with me without being mature enough to come discuss the issue. I release them from my life. Now, father I thank you for the true connections that you have in store for my life. The kind that will outlive lies, rumors, and scandals. I appreciate you that you would not leave me in the dark but that you would take the time to reveal the true intent of man's heart. Father most of all I thank you that you give me the strength and courage to not cut ties with any persons that I have an assignment for before its time. In doing this I could finish my course and be done in Jesus' name. I thank you for your truth. I thank you for your concern. Keep my tongue from destroying the very thing that wants to destroy me. If you say build, help me. If you say encourage that very one, help me. If you say be kind, please help me. In Jesus' mighty name I pray. Amen.

Chapter 11

Persecution

I remember living in some part of Georgia. I was fresh out of high school and I was excited about leaving my parents' house to go adventure life without them. The only problem was that the college that I attended did not have dormitories at the time of my attendance. My parents did not want me living on my own because they felt that I was not age-appropriate. I remember my mom receiving a phone call from a Pastor that was under the spiritual covering of my Pastor at the time. They had just moved to the same area that I was going to attend college. They had a house that was directly across the street from the school and only 10 minutes walking distance. They had an extra room and offered my mom an open door to allow me to come in to stay with them. We thought this had to be ordained by God. I was just a month away from the start of school and a way was made for me to stay somewhere safe. The agreement was that I would stay with the Pastors for 1 year and then get my own apartment. I was happy to go stay with the Pastors, I was also happy to leave so that I could have my own space. I am a very private person and having my own space is a big deal for me. I had a couple of friends that knew just how private I was and would often ask me how was I going to get married. I would ask them what they meant on how was I going to get married? I said, "You just say yes to the person you feel you are to be with." Lol. They would say well you would not be getting married because you are too private. Marriage is about opening your life and sharing your space with someone else. Ummm.... That was over 10 years ago. Maybe that was a curse that they said over me because I'm not married to this day. Lol. Maybe I should send it back. Lol. I understood what they were saying and to be honest marriage was not on my mind at the time and for some reason, it's not on my mind now that I'm over 25 years old. Lol. I must say that I am content and honestly feel that when God is ready for me to marry, I will. However, my mind is preoccupied with other projects at this time. Anyway, when I moved into my apartment I felt a sense of greater freedom, this is not in any way to say that I was bound living with the Pastors. They were loving and nurturing people. It was more of me being able to do what I wanted to do whenever I wanted to do it. If I felt like waking up around 2 a.m. to pray aloud then I could do that without being a disruption to anyone else.

Let's get to the point of what this section is all about, which is persecution. What is the meaning of Persecution? After viewing an article written by Reverend Billy Graham, persecution means to oppress, harass and also to bring to judgment or punishment. It was around my 2nd year at the Community College of Georgia. I had started out at a community college to see if schooling was for me. Years later I finally realized that it was. I graduated. Lol! I developed a heavy prayer life at an early age. Praying had become innate to me. It was what I did early in the mornings and would often set a time to do in the evenings. To be honest I would actually pray inwardly all day. I would pray over the water that I drink, the food that I ate, the church services that I attended, the church services that I was invited to preach or to minister in song, over my family, and for my enemies. I would pray about all things. Aside from Jesus, prayer was and still is the foundation of my very existence.

One day after class I had come home for my lunch break. I was fasting 6 A.M.-6 P.M. either for that day or for that week. I had purposed in my heart during that early morning prayer to come home and pray again for lunch. I think this was around the time that I had lost roughly 20lbs because of my fasting schedule. I was praying during that noon hour and the Lord had taken me into a clear vision. I must say that when you eat light naturally and pray a lot it will not take long before you are traveling through the secret places with God. Prophetically I had come through the womb of a woman by the name of Dr. Paulette Olasoji. The Lord would use her and a young man by the name of Apostolic Bishop Tevin Roberts. It did not matter what their assignment was they would produce God's glory. From saying a congregational prayer to preaching the unadulterated word of God, they would produce the glory of the Lord at a high level. While being raised in her spiritual house, she and Apostolic Bishop Tevin Roberts would instill into all their congregants the importance of prayer and living the fasted life. God reveals a lot to righteous, praying and consecrated people. It had not been 5 minutes before the Lord had snatched my spirit to where He needed it to be in the spirit. I will write a short book soon called, "Easy Passage Ways into The Vision Realm." I had once heard messages by the late Kathryn Kulman and Dr. Myles Munroe on how God would do great things through vessels that would fast and pray. Not only was I able to read about it, but I was able to witness it through the lives of Chief Apostle Dr. Paulette Jones Olasoji and Apostolic Bishop Tevin Roberts. Please allow me to say that greatness is not how great a crowd you stand before, the loudness of your voice or how well everyone knows your name. Greatness is how well you stand in faith and how effective your doings are. If any person is being blessed through your works, then you are considered great my friend. When I went into that vision, the Lord had taken my spirit back on campus and I was putting up signs to start a gospel choir. I heard the voice of the Lord also speak into my spirit, "Go start a CCGC choir." I would like to interject this piece of information in that when you are called into the prophetic ministry God will give you assignments along the way to train you how to be obedient at His every command. Your whole ministry will be shaped through great faith and obedience to God. After I had come out of the vision, I questioned the Lord. I said, "Lord are you sure you want me to do that." I must take time to testify here in this moment. If the Lord would impress for me to do anything for Him, I would always feel incomplete if my pastor did not bless it first. I would always share with my leaders things I was planning to do before I did them. In my opinion, this was to ensure that no one had any grounds to say that I was operating under a renegade spirit. A renegade is someone that runs wild in the earth without any supervision or guidance. Should anyone rise up to ask who my leaders were I would always be able to point to where they were. Now that I am older, I understand that when the Lord says anything it is already blessed. You will grow to know that whether your leaders bless your assignments or not, if God said to do it then He will be with you and "it." Yes, there are times that God will give you vision that will incorporate your local assembly. However, there are other tasks that He will give you that may not necessarily be for the whole church to accomplish but they will certainly be welcomed to join in to support. Selah!

After I had shared with my Pastor what the vision of starting the choir was she gave her blessings. I began my journey. I created fliers. I went to the office of the Campus Recreation Director to speak with Dave Hines. Here is another developmental strategy that the Lord will use to get you prepared for your journey and that is to speak to people in high places. God will purposefully give you a task to do that will require you to speak to leadership persons and to ask for their help. This is a way for Him to break all pride that you may have and to shift your thinking from believing that you will be able to do this assignment alone.

I had passed Dave a few times on campus and we would always speak to one another. I was nervous. I went in and was asked to sit down. Mr. Dave asked me to explain my vision. You must understand that this was no secular event that I was proposing but a spiritual one. I felt like Moses having to go release the Lord's words to a pharaoh. Out of my mouth came a bold, "Mr. Dave, I feel that we should start a college choir and in 6 weeks I want to have a gospel choir concert." To my surprise, Mr. Hines leaned forward in his chair, smiled and asked how he could be of my assistance. Mr. Dave had asked me to give him a budget and that he would back me up. "Wow!" I thought. I asked for his permission to post fliers across the campus, to use the campus microphone and sound system and to use the student center. Mr. Dave gave his full support. After I had put up the fliers, I had received a few calls of interest about the choir. Both African American and Caucasians had joined. We had grown to 9 members and would have rehearsals every week. When the campus leaders of the different clubs knew that we had a choir we would be asked to sing. I was in the Collegiate Baptist Campus bible study and they would ask us to sing a song occasionally. As time would progress the Lord started to give me dreams about the people in the choir. He started allowing me to have insight on the areas of their struggle. However, it was this one particular guy that I kept seeing in my dreams. He was not a part of the choir but had some kind of relationship with the people that had joined. Please stop! I know what you might be thinking, "Oh you must have liked him?" No this was not the case. The Lord kept blowing his face up before me and I saw him trying to kill me in some way. I did not understand it fully. This was because whenever I would see him on campus he would speak. He was popular. He was an ordained minister of the gospel. He was nice. So I continued on loving and doing what I knew I was called to do. There was a girl that everyone kept telling me about. The people in the choir would often say, "Ashley! You need to meet Sara." There was this black history program that one of the campus clubs had put on and she was to sing at this event. Some of the choir members asked what my class schedule was like because they wanted to take me to the event. It worked out that the event was during lunch hour. They were serving lunch so that worked out because I would get a chance to hear Sara sing and I would get free lunch! When Sara was called she seemed a little nervous. However, she talked a little before singing and that helped to break that nervousness. She opened her mouth and sang the song," Summertime" by the famous Ella Fitzgerald. The girl nailed it. I mean she sang the song justly. Not only could she sing but she was pleasant off stage. She had a smile that would light up any dark day. After the event, the choir members that had brought me to the event introduced me to Sara. The first thing that the members said was, "Sara, this is Ashley she started a choir and you should join it." Sara smiled and simply said, "Ooook!" Lol. We all stayed around to encourage Sara on what a wonderful job she had done singing. I had to leave to get to my class that was about to start in 20 minutes. Sara and I agreed to meet back in the student center later in the week. I believe it was on Thursday night after my English class that prophetess Brown and I was headed to the student center. Sara had not made it to the center yet. Prophetess Brown and I stayed and talked about the Word and the issues of life. We laughed and made jokes about some of the tactics the enemy would try to throw our way. Sara came in on our conversation and joined in. We were able to talk more about the choir and what we wanted to do for the concert. I had heard that she was good with voices and teaching parts. I had asked her if she would join and she said that she would ask her parents. She was raised in a very strict house. Her grandparents were pastors in the city and her parents were ministers of music. She had a major part to play in the music department of her church and she wanted to be sure that joining the campus choir wouldn't impede upon her church duties. We all kept chatting. Sara began to talk about how her parents had a community choir and did a concert every year. She asked if I would be interested in stopping by the church to check out the choir and to meet her parents. We exchanged numbers. The rehearsals were on Monday nights. I did not have a night class so I was able to go check out the choir.

When I went in, I remember a woman walking from the front of the church to the back of the church to greet me. She asked who I was. I said with a big smile on my face, "Hello I'm Ashley!" she then went on to say, "Oh ok. Yes, my daughter had told us that you were coming." The mother had escorted me to the choir stand. She waited for the others to show up before starting. She began to ask questions about where I was from and how long I was living in Brunswick Georgia. Sara and a majority of the members had come in. We all greeted one another. We all had to sing to audition. I had a song in my back pocket. When my turn had come to audition, I sang a familiar song entitled "More Than Anything." This song is known in the African American church and was written by Lamar Campbell. Everyone loved my audition. The choir directors loved my voice so much that they had given me a song to lead for the concert. A person had come in the door. It was the same guy that the Lord had been showing me in my dreams and vision. Everyone was happy to see him. I thought wow he is popular here too. He came in and once again he greeted me very kindly. After that night of auditioning and being told what the vision of their concert was, we were told to go home and think about if it would be something that we could dedicate our efforts, time and talents to.

During the week I resumed with focusing on the college campus rehearsals and preparations for the college concert. Though it was months away I have always been a believer in taking the necessary time to prepare for something. This would ensure that the event would not look like it was thrown together but that the necessary time was put into the work. Well by the time I had realized it, it was Monday again. It was time to go tell the community choir if I had chosen to be a part of their work or not. I thought that I should be apart. After all, this would have been a great opportunity for me to learn from two people on how to conduct concerts. When I had gone to the church that night, I had to sit outside for a few minutes. After a while, some other cars pulled up and we waited and chatted until the leaders had arrived. Everything was going great in both my choir on campus and with the community choir. We all seemed to be focused and would come with one purpose in mind, which was to sing. As time passed we were still progressing really well. Our choir directors were nice but firm. They wouldn't move onto another part of the song until we had the sound down perfectly. I loved it. I was learning so much. The tips that I would learn from the community choir I would teach them to the college choir. I had started developing good relationships with everyone in the choir.

To make a very long story short there was this young man that had been known by a lot of people in the community, church arena, and the college. People liked him and so did I. He seemed very personable. We would talk briefly from time to time. When I joined the community choir in the city to my surprise he also joined and became apart. I was happy to see so many other young folks come out to be apart of the work of the Lord. As time went on, we were given a list of songs to learn and I found out that I was to lead a song. As dedicated as I was to my own choir practices I would be just as dedicated to attending the community choir practice. Some more time had passed by and things were getting a little shaky. The Lord had started using me privately to reveal the hidden things that were in some peoples lives and to pray with them. The people started to tell others around the campus about me so that people started asking if they could set up meetings to meet me because they had wanted to talk about some things that were going on in their lives. The Lord knew my heart and how I was not prophesying to people so that they could spread my name around campus but only because I felt a burden to do so.

Well, I remember receiving a phone call from one of the members of the community choir. I remember him being a little scared to speak with me, but I encouraged him to express himself. This was one of the choir members that would come to my house, we would go out to eat, go to church services together- he was a good guy. We would laugh all the time. However, I could tell that something was troubling his spirit. He said, "Sis, I need to warn you about something that is happening with this community choir." He went on to expose how he had received a phone call from the members of the choir to invite him to come to the church because they were having a meeting. I said to him, "Ok." He said sis but the meeting was about you. I said, "Oh, I see." He then revealed how the guy that everyone liked and loved so much was telling people that I was a witch that worked witchcraft and that I was spreading rumors against that ministry. I expressed to him that the Lord had been dealing with me about that guy for some time. He said sis I just wanted to tell you that I got your back and that I will not be in attendance. We then laughed about the whole thing and decided to go out to eat. I then understood what the Lord was showing me with this guy trying to kill me. God was revealing that he was trying to kill my name and character before people that liked me. The sad thing was that it worked with quite a few of them. Lol.

This is just one of a myriad of things that I have gone through. However, the persecution was my sign that I was doing something right. The devil was mad and upset that I was influencing people on the campus and wanted to stop that flow. I want to encourage someone that you can not take your warfare personal. The rumors were not about me, but it was a direct attack against the work of God in the region. I often tell people that they will need to learn to read their warfare correctly. A sign of immaturity is when you start to fight back with the intent to secure your name. We were never called to defend our name but rather to defend this gospel. I believe that when you continuously live upright before the Lord, your lifestyle will fight for you. This was days before the concert. Believe it or not I still went to the concert, sang my song, and left. I killed all of that with love and with the anointing of the Lord.

Some years had passed by and I was contacted by this same guy that spread the rumor. He sought to tell me why he did what he did. He told me that he was jealous and that he just could not figure me out. He admitted that people would come to him with the things that God told me to tell them and how it was true. He said he could not tolerate other people magnifying another person. Remind you he was used to being looked up too. He was a minister, but God showed me how he was living a secret homosexual lifestyle. He admitted that he did not believe that I could be young and really live right. He said that he thought that I was into witchcraft to be able to tell all those people about themselves. I became offended all over again in that moment, but God helped me control myself. I saw how that this was an opportunity to minister to this young minister that God was able to keep anything that desired to be kept. I laid down my offense and believed God to help me minister to the young man. By the end of the conversation he apologized, and we were able to move beyond this dilemma.

My point is that God allowed an opportunity for me to die to myself through persecution. I could have told him off and came out of character. When elevation is near, you will often find yourself in some sort of test where your stand for Christ is being challenged. God will allow for you to undergo great fire and heat for the sake of perfecting you. As a leader in any capacity you do not have the liberty to react the way you want to act. You cannot respond the way you want to respond. It will also be a trying time because God will give you a good word to share with the very one that tried to kill you. Isn't that something! I had to give a word to the very one that was used of the devil to destroy some of my good connections. Lord have mercy. But I want to encourage somebody that this may be hard for you. Yes, it is difficult, but God is able to get you through it. Remember it is not what they do that you will be held accountable for, but it is what you do and what you say. Have I always been this way, no. I had to grow to this point and am still growing to this day. However, this brother caught me in a good season. Lol.

Prayer:

Father in Jesus name persecution does not rub the skin right. If not careful it can produce a heart of hatred, un-forgiveness, and bitterness. Father I am human and being mistreated by any person is offensive to me. Father because it is offensive to me help me to handle it in a way that will not bring great reproach against your name or give validation to the misconceptions said of me. Help me to see persecution as a sign of elevation. Keep my tongue and my attitude right. Cause me not to entertain the spirit of revenge. Help me to remember that Jesus went through it. He was called the son of Beelzebub. The disciples went through it. They were rebels. When I see it throughout this life help me and the rest of my brothers and sisters in Christ to remain true representatives of you. Father, I thank you for victory in every season. In Jesus mighty name. Amen.

Chapter 12

Axle

I have trained myself to get up for 5 a.m. prayer whether it was with a corporate body of believers or within the confinements of my home. As I sit and write I think back over 10 years of striving to be disciplined in my prayer life. On the morning of 1-23-2019, I had gotten up to pray. After my prayer time, I went back to sleep and had a dream of one of my deceased Granddads. Grandad Lawrence Reynolds Sr. had just recently passed right before Christmas in December of 2018. In this short dream, it was him, another guy and myself. My granddad was talking to this other guy about an axel and about being level headed in this life. He turned towards me and was saying how this is what this next generation needed and that was to have the right axel and to be more level headed. This really threw me for a loop. I didn't understand exactly what he was saying to me. When I came out of the dream, I began to research what an axel was and its significance. I also began to look at what being level-headed meant for the context of this dream. While on my search I came across a definition for axel through the Merriam Webster Dictionary website. According to Webster, axle means a fixed bar or beam with bearings at its ends on which wheels (as of a cart) revolve. There are several types of axles. There are rear, front and stub axles. According to research and my understanding these three types of axles covers every aspect of the moving vehicles. Well, after reading about axles I still had not been able to draw a conclusion of what my granddad was trying to convey to me in that dream. I pondered for a few days on the information that I had read. Finally, I decided to go see Mr. Peterson. Mr. Peterson is a science teacher that was in the hall next to where my workstation. I sat at my desk and decided to take a little walk. I was on planning period. On my way I felt an excitement because I thought that Mr. Peterson was going to give me my answer. I arrived to Mr. Peterson's door and knocked. One of his students opened the door and welcomed me into their space. I walked in with a smile on my face. As I walked towards Mr. Peterson he had a facial expression that would say, "Oh my goodness, I wonder what she is going to ask today?" If anyone knows me they know that

I like to pick their brains by asking questions. I leaned over Mr. Peterson's desk and said, "Hi, may I ask you a question?" Mr. Peterson just looked with great amazement of what I was going to ask. "Yes!" said Mr. Peterson. I went on to state my question, "You see, Mr. Peterson I need to know exactly what the purpose of an axle is." I went on to say, "It may seem a little weird but even though I had spent some time repetitively reviewing the definition of axle, I still do not know how to apply it to real life situations." I went on to say, "Is the purpose of an axle to be the stabilizing component which enables the wheels to keep in motion?" Mr. Peterson said, "well, let's look over the definition." He then pulled up the remotely same definition that I had pulled up. Mr. Peterson then stated, "Yes, your understanding is correct. The axle is a rod that enables wheels to rotate." We both smiled and I went my way. I smiled because I realized that I had come into the understanding ever since the day before. I then took this understanding and applied it to what my Granddad had said in the dream. I came to the conclusion that because the axle is the rod of stability which helps the wheels continue on with motion, my granddad was saying that we need to invite the force of stability into our lives so that we will continue on moving towards our desired destination. All of us have a destination but we absolutely cannot get there if we are not connected to a steady and vital piece that will ensure movement in the right direction. Jesus Christ is the rod of stability. If we would take the time to invite Jesus in and keep Him at the center of our everyday activities we too will be steady. Let us define what stability means. According to Webster's dictionary, stability means the strength to stand or endure. The purpose of a wheel is to turn on an axle and create motion in one direction. Without the axle the wheels would be bouncing in more than one direction. This can be viewed as instability. I believe that it is the will of the Lord that we be headed only in the one direction that He has ordained for our lives in every season of our lives. The axle will ensure this for us. When hardships, trouble and trials come our way we still have a responsibility to remain steady. That's right, we still have a mandate from the Lord to carry out. I remember the words of a mighty man of valor in the person of Apostle Tevin Roberts say, "In every season we still must produce." To be unshakeable while under great pressure calls for one to be mentally strong.

James 1:2-4

Count it all joy, my brothers, when you meet trials of various kinds, ³for you know that the testing of your faith produces steadfastness. ⁴And let steadfastness have its full effect, that you may be perfect and complete, lacking in nothing.

Living in this life we can be sure to face long seasons of difficulties, pain, disappointments, setbacks, persecutions, trials, etc. The people that have been through very hard times but have made it out have testified that it was contributed to them being connected in some way to the Rock of Ages, Jesus Christ. When they felt as though they would break, crack or crumble while going through rough seasons, they could always depend on God to keep them steered in the right direction. I can surely testify that when going through hard times my thoughts would surely undergo severe attacks. I would hear thoughts such as, you're stupid, you're not good enough, and no one cares for you. I would also hear a taunting voice in the back of my mind telling me to stop wasting my time serving the Lord and go enjoy myself with the pleasures of this life. Oh yes, that demonic voice would try to steer me in the direction of which my flesh would be most gratified. That's just it! The devil would never tell you to go do something that you wouldn't find pleasing. I would start thinking things like maybe I should go get some wine, go to a club, go on a dating spree (bouncing from person to person), etc. However, because my roots in Christ are deep, I did not do any of these things though the thoughts were strong. Instead I would cry, sing, go to church, dance in the privacy of my home, laugh, watch television shows that would make me laugh, go to the movies, go to a restaurant and invite a person with whose company I would enjoy, or go riding around town. In other words, I would leave the atmosphere where the devil would speak so heavily into my ears. I would purposefully gravitate towards places where I knew my spirit would be lifted. I feel led to encourage someone reading this book right now. Never stay in the place where the enemy is talking loudly to you, especially if you are vulnerable and are considering the suggestions. Remember that he will never suggest you do something that you would not become addicted to afterwards.

Shall we Pray?

Father in the name of Jesus, someone may be reading this and thinking, "Oh this is me!" Father I ask that you become that axle in our lives.Father in times of difficulty and when we feel less than human,encourage our hearts. Oh God when the enemy of our soul comes to invade the territory of our minds, arrest our thoughts and allow us to stay on the path set for our lives. Oh God that we would always look to you for strength and stability. May we never fall to the set traps of Satan. Father, may you cause us to confuse the enemy and all of hell by becoming stable and keeping focus. Father, I thank you that in every season we are victorious. In Jesus' mighty name. Amen!

I got it! I understand what my grandfather meant about having an axle in our lives. Though I have viewed myself as being stable and able to maintain under pressure, I think my grandad was telling me that if we are going to make it through purpose and towards destiny on this earth we would need to keep Jesus as the axle in our everyday lives. Yes we would need to allow for Jesus to be the center of it all. When times of trouble would arise we would not be easily swayed, tossed and driven but that we would remain a constant while on this journey called life. I remember my mother, who is a wonderful woman, sharing a Scripture with me. This Scripture was found in

Matthew 11:7

As John's disciples were leaving, Jesus began to speak to the crowds about John: "What did you go out into the wilderness to see? A reed swaying in the wind?

This Scripture spoke volumes to my very soul. John was a mighty prophet in the sight of the Lord. He was very unique and was not controlled by the traditions of his era. Jesus asked the question, "Exactly what did you all come out to see? A weak prophet?" Jesus was essentially saying that John was in no way frail, easily swayed or easily to give up. Jesus assured the crowd that if you ever needed a strong leader to look to, you could surely look at John. John went up under great tribulations and trials and was eventually beheaded because of his unwillingness to bend or bow. While under great pressure John did the Scripture which said to be steadfast, immovable and always abiding in the work of the Lord Knowing that thy labor was not in vain. God was John's axle and he helped him to remain steady even when it got rough. John stayed the course because He knew that his labor was not in vain and that one day God would repay him for every persecution, failure, rejection, hurt, pain, discomfort, loneliness and even murder. John kept on going because he was working towards something far greater than what he could visibly see. Let us become like John and see the bigger picture.

"Let Jesus make you strong, secure and steady by becoming your axle!"

Chapter 13

Level-Headed

The other part of the dream with my Grandad was that he said this generation needed to be more level-headed. According to Webster being level-headed means that you have the ability to remain calm under all circumstances. It takes no rocket scientist to predict that if all is going good in a person's life that he or she will be calm. If their bills are being paid, they have food, water, shelter, health,money in the bank, tactful relationships and able to do some shopping, they would be calm. There are no external or internal stressors that would cause for them to be upset. Nothing in their lives are in disarray.

What happens when all hell breaks loose in your life? Are you able to remain organized? How do you handle life and the people in your life when things start to go contrary to what you expected? How is your decision making process? Great leaders are able to work well while under stress. They have a vision and they have goals. They set their face like flint and move in the direction of their calling.

Hebrews 12:2

We do this by keeping our eyes on Jesus, the champion who initiates and perfects our faith. Because of the joy awaiting him, he endured the cross, disregarding its shame. Now he is seated in the place of honor beside God's throne.

Jesus knew that his end would not be the seat of shame and embarrassment but the seat of honor. He knew that the keys of faith and his obedience concerning his earthly assignment would be reached if he just would not give up in hard times. If you would take the time to read Matthew 26:36-46, you would see that just moments before he would enter into the last stages of ministry it seemed as though the Father was not with him and neither any of his friends or disciples. If you ask me that is when the greatest level of support and encouragement is needed, right before the last stage. This is the stage where the heat is turned all the way up and if there has ever been a time that a Word of encouragement was needed or support was needed it would have been then. To have God or someone tell you to hold on just a little while longer would have been sufficient. However, if we read we would find that when Jesus prays to the father he answered him not a word. When Jesus went to check on the three disciples they were sleep and not alert. Oh the thoughts that ran through Jesus' mind and the feelings of disgust that ran through his emotions. However, I would like to look at this Scripture in a different light.

John 10:30

"I and the Father are one."

I would like to submit that when Jesus went to pray and he heard no spoken words could it be that it was no need to call on God because he was right there with him in the trial. God did possibly answer Jesus' cry by helping Him not to give in. Jesus had opened up a portion of his grief and sorrow to Peter, James, and John with these words *found in*

Matthew 26:38

Then he said to them, "My soul is overwhelmed with sorrow to the point of death. Stay here and keep watch with me."

God answered him by giving him the strength that he needed despite how abandoned he felt by the Father and despite him having a poor intercession team. God did not let Jesus' will be led by a lie in that He helped Jesus to still say, "Yes!" Emotions and perspective are two components which contribute to why people throw in the towel and quit. Yes, we must monitor how we feel about what we see. However, one key component that leaders have is that they do not start anything without first counting the cost. Another proof of God answering Jesus was that after going back into the garden to pray the third time he returned and then he said, "Rise, let us GO!"

Matthew 26: 45-46

[45]Then he returned to the disciples and said to them, "Are you still sleeping and resting? Look, the hour has come, and the Son of Man is delivered into the hands of sinners. [46]Rise! Let us go! Here comes my betrayer!"

Coming out of prayer and finding his team sleep while he was in a critical moment of his life had to be hard for Jesus. He must have felt dejected and not cared for. But watch how God blesses Jesus' perspective in that he says,

Matthew 26:41

The spirit is willing, but the flesh is weak.

This was God helping Jesus to understand that these people just could not help their lack of support. The assignment was just too great for them to handle. Sometimes we take along the ones who we think are strong enough when in reality they may be strong for help with some things, but not all things. The other understanding that I got was that Jesus was really praying himself through this dark hour. I would like to think that sometimes God had to put your intercessors to sleep less you start to believe that you can only make it through if they pray. No, the bible teaches us that Jesus prayed. He prayed and found them sleep. Some of the greatest gifts that God can give us is that he puts our natural help to sleep. We then have the opportunity to be introduced to the level power, strength, vigor, tenacity and determination that lies within. As long as they are praying we incapacitate ourselves from seeing what treasures lie within and that we have the ability through God to reach Him.

Luke 14:28

For which of you, intending to build a tower, sitteth not down first, and counteth the cost, whether he have sufficient to finish it?

The enemy's desire is to make you get so full of ambition until you are not sensible. His desire is that you start a God ordained idea in the folly of your mind. This would ensure that you fail. Before failing in the physical we first fail in our minds. When we choose to take left or wrong turns in life, it is because our mind has been paralyzed from doing what is right. When something is paralyzed it no longer has the ability to function properly, thus we make rash decisions. Your greatest weapon to defeat the devil is not through acts of flesh.

Ephesians 6:12

For our struggle is not against flesh and blood, but against the rulers, against the authorities, against the powers of this dark world and against the spiritual forces of evil in the heavenly realms.

Your greatest weapon to defeat Satan aside from the name of Jesus and his blood is COMPLETION. The devil hates finishers.

Yes, he despises those that have learned how to go through the pains and agony of giving birth to vision without succumbing to it.

Right road. Wrong time. Wait your turn.

Isaiah 40:31 Amplified Bible (AMP)

But those who wait for the Lord [who expect, look for, and hope in Him], Will gain new strength and renew their power; They will lift up their wings [and rise up close to God] like eagles [rising toward the sun]; They will run and not become weary, They will walk and not grow tired.

I hear Isaiah 40:31 in my spirit. I was riding home from a very prestigious interview. I had a dream of myself applying for a certain position with a specific company. I questioned God and then applied. Anybody besides me ever wondered why God chose you to go a certain route that seemed outside of your capabilities? The fact is that God does this to reveal another revelation of who we are to ourselves. He looks at us from a different perspective. When man tries to stunt your spirit, that always seems to be the time when God steps in to lift you in your very soul. The first time I had an interview for this particular job I was not chosen. It shook my faith. My faith was challenged because I literally saw myself apply for this job and then saw my paper work with the words written across it, "Hired!" When it did not happen I felt like God did not live up to His word. I was encouraging other people while feeling like this same God could not help me. 4 months had passed since I was denied the position. I received an email that offered me the opportunity to re-apply but in another department. The interview went well. Lots of laughter was in the atmosphere. The manager just happened to be from Savannah, GA, which is my hometown. This allowed for us to be a little freer with one another. I was riding home and made a turn onto a street that was a little congested. I did not notice it at first, but the car lineup was a little heavier than usual. It was so piled up with cars until my GPS had to remind me that even though I was on the right route, traffic was a little heavier. As I began to move along at a very slow pace the Holy Spirit began to bring to my attention the green light. Though I could see the green light and other cars were moving forward,I was still about 15 cars behind. The Holy Spirit spoke to me and simply said, "Rejoice!" I was wondering why I should be rejoicing about being behind in a line of cars. I was reminded that though I was behind other cars and moving slowly that I still had the green light and that I was still moving along. It is possible to be on the right path, but it not be your turn yet. Let me explain. I was in that long line of cars where the green light was flashing, however, while it was the turn for selective cars to turn at that time it was not my turn. I was approaching the season of my turn. This can be one of the most difficult times in the waiting process. Seeing that green light causes many people to think that they should be able to just glide into their desired placed at that moment. The reality is that seeing that green light is just the confirmation, or the encouragement needed to keep you aware that you are almost to the place of your destination. It did not matter how impatient I had become while waiting for my "turn," I had to come to accept the fact that someone was in front of me and I just had to wait. I must confess that seeing that green light helped my perspective that in just a short while I too would make that "turn."

Let us pray: Prayer for Patience

Dear heavenly Father, you are in heaven and I am on earth. Therefore, Father I acknowledge that you see all things from a higher dimension. Father I honor you because you are wise and all knowing. You are honest and loving. So, Father I come to you in all honesty. I am struggling in the area of patience. Yes according to Galatians 5:22, patience should be resting in me and operating through but the reality is that I am tired of hearing the word wait. I am struggling with waiting my turn. However, Father, I know that you are able to keep me even in this season of distress. I acknowledge that you are able to encourage this area of my life that keeps me wanting something before my time. So, Father, in the name of Jesus I bind this spirit of impatience and I loose the spirit of forbearance and faithfulness right where I am. I command that I will not have a wandering eye which wanders off into the affairs of others but that I will focus on that which you have right before me. Father, when I finally arrive to my place of promise I will bless you even the more. In Jesus' mighty name. Amen.

Chapter 14

Slander

Psalms 101:5

Whoever slanders his neighbor secretly I will destroy. Whoever has a haughty look and an arrogant heart I will not endure.

Slander. What can I really say about it? I was not going to write about this in this book, however, I received a text from my dad about slander. Wow, maybe I was supposed to write about this spirit and to encourage those who are faced with it from day to day. If you are going to live in this world and decide in your heart to do anything worthwhile, you are going to experience this vile spirit. According to Webster, slander is defined as the utterance of false charges or misrepresentations which defame and damage another's reputation. I would not dare give credit to the enemy of my very soul but I will shine light on this cruel and evil spirit, which prowls with vicious intent to discredit the good that you represent. Throughout my life, I have been met with this sneaky yet powerful spirit. Meeting people is not a problem for me. The problem is that I have come across some that have sought to destroy my very name. Not that I am so much, but I do believe the bible in that it states:

Proverbs 22:1

Choose a good reputation over great riches; being held in high esteem is better than silver or gold.

The word of God clearly admonishes us that we live in such a way that for our namesake we have no spoken faults against us proven to be true.

1 Peter 3:16

Having a good conscience, so that, when you are slandered, those who revile your good behavior in Christ may be put to shame.

I have and am still striving to live my life unto the glory of the Lord. Since the tender age of 15, I have given my life to the Lord. Not to say that I am perfect but as they would say in the old Holiness churches, "I mean heaven and heaven all the way." I have tried to treat people with common decency but it literally looked like the sweeter I got, the more they talked. The funny thing about slander is that it really is just one's opinion. It is the mind of one towards another. How one sees another is projected upon those that do not know another. The ignorant part about slander is that people will excommunicate you based upon the corruptible perverse thoughts of another which has no grounds for accuracy. So people have chosen to hate one based upon a lie. This is ignorance. I once heard a prophet refer to slander as hatred on a buddy pass. Throughout my life I have had people come to apologize to me because they felt guilty about partaking in the slander directed towards me. They would admit that they did not like me because of another person's ill feelings towards me. This spirit of slander will seek to detach you away from persons that mean you good or those who hold you in high esteem. This spirit operates by stealth and is very sneaky in its approach. It gains its power by having some type of access to you. It seeks out information about you. It typically looks for your weaknesses so that it may exploit you. It tells you to your face how wonderful you are and how great a blessing you are. In actuality, it hates your very existence and wants you dead (spiritually). Not only does it want access to you but also it will seek attachment to those that you have had good relationships with. This is all a part of the set up. Because the root of these tactics is jealousy, it seeks to drop seeds of negativity in those who you know. The ones who would potentially help you get to your next level; it seeks to turn their hearts sour towards you. It seeks to strip you of your help. Oh, this demon is heartless. It will see you being embraced and accepted by others and start trying to find ways to impede the favor that you receive from such ones. It may work with a few, but the connections that matter God will sustain them.

Isaiah 54:17

No weapon formed against you shall prosper, And every tongue which rises against you in judgment You shall condemn. This is the heritage of the servants of the Lord, And their righteousness is from Me, says the Lord.

The Lord had given me a revelation in that for any person that would allow for a spirit of slander to influence them in any way towards you was never really for you in the beginning. You really could thank the person operating in slander because they really just helped you to identify who is genuinely for you and who is not. You see it was just like what Joseph said, "It was meant for my bad but God will turn it around for my good." This spirit of slander though it is working against you, is actually working for you because any persons that would dare side with its evil intentions true heart is being exposed.

Luke 21:36

Watch ye therefore, and pray always, that ye may be accounted worthy to escape all these things that shall come to pass, and to stand before the Son of man.

Jesus knew who was in his circle. He was not ignorant that the majority of them did not know him and that there was a devil amongst them all. Anytime a person enters your life you must pray and ask the Lord why that person is in your life. You must be intentional even in your relationships. Not everybody is meant to know you on an intimate level. They are only to know you for business purposes, work purposes, or ministry purposes. Let me park right here and help someone realize that yes you may have been called to work with someone for the work of ministry but it does not signify that you all are to walk together on any level beyond that. Know the purpose for all of your relationships. I feel led to prophesy right here that,

"God is going to give you a revelation on all of your relationships. I declare unto you that you will know the purpose, intent and the spirit behind every connection. In Jesus' mighty name."

May every snake that slithers in your life be caught in Jesus' mighty name. I say unto you as the Lord spoke unto me in that he would choose all of your connections. I pray that you stop trying to pick whom you should be with for whatever purpose under heaven. I pray that you will rest in God almighty and allow Him to locate your help.

Prayer:

May you not be confused in your relationships. May you walk into every connection with strong and high discernment. May you be spiritual enough to separate your help from those that come to hurt and hinder the work of the Lord. May all of your enemies be exposed and may every plan of the spirit of slander fail now in Jesus' name. May you walk in the sweet fellowship of the Holy Spirit and enjoy the benefits of waiting on God to choose your company. May corrupt company never deceive you. May God bring you true company. May your company be filled with the wisdom and knowledge of God to do an unshakable work for Christ the Lord.

Chapter 15

Too Precious for "That"

I had a vision of a young woman who had become ill. She had noticed that some changes occurred in her female organs. The enemy really had her worried. She still had her menstrual cycle. She was still able to urinate, but there was some pain in her urination. Her urine had a strong fishy smell that would travel for miles. Whenever she went out she would not use the restroom for fear that the smell would offend those around her. She was experiencing some itching and irritation. She was young and inexperienced with dealing with a UTI (urinary tract infection.) I saw how the enemy was using her worries about her vaginal irritations as a way to inflict fear that possibly she had some sort of vaginal cancer. She was worried and called someone close to her that was a nurse to get some advice. Her advisor prompted her to go see a doctor because it sounded like either a UTI or a yeast infection. The young lady put her fears away and went to see a doctor. After seeing a doctor and having some tests done, the young lady was informed that she had developed a UTI. She was both disturbed and relieved. She was disturbed because she did not know how she had gotten the UTI, but relieved to know that it was not cancer or any other serious condition. She gave God the praise. She asked the doctor how she got the UTI and surprisingly the doctor found tracks of tea in her system. She said, "I got this from tea. Huh! Well I'm not drinking tea anymore." That doctor laughed and explained to her that it was not that she could not have tea, but the tea she did drink was dirty and had too much sugar in it. He explained that her body was trying to find a way to reject it. She found it funny because the only place that she drank tea was at her job. She vowed to not drink tea from her job again. Funny vision right?

It was days later that the Holy Spirit had reminded me of what I saw and began to give me understanding. He showed me that young lady's body and then showed me a pitcher of dirty tea. The Holy Spirit helped me to know that the young lady's body represented the Body of Christ. The pitcher of dirty tea was a representative of damaged, spoiled and insufficient substance. I was being taught on how fragile and precious the body is and how it cannot take in food and drink that is not sufficient for the caliber of living that God has called it to. The result of taking in insufficient food is that one will become sick and the body is unable to function at maximum capacity. The Lord spoke to me and simply helped me to know that we the people of God cannot afford to pull up to everyone's table. Let us look at a Scripture:

Ezekiel 2:8-9 New Revised Standard Version (NRSV)

8 But you, mortal, hear what I say to you; do not be rebellious like that rebellious house; open your mouth and eat what I give you. 9 I looked, and a hand was stretched out to me, and a written scroll was in it.

Just as the prophet Ezekiel was prompted by the Lord to be selective in what he ate, we too must be careful of what we eat. When we eat food that is filled with chemicals and other ingredients that our body cannot handle, we risk becoming sick with some sort of manifested disease. So it is in the spirit. When we eat from spiritual foreign tables, it can result in spiritual illness and/or

death. Let us look at the story of the young
prophet who ate from a foreign table.

*Ezekiel   13:15-23-   New   International
Version (NIV)*

*15 So the prophet said to him, "Come home
with me and eat."*

*16 The man of God said, "I cannot turn
back and go with you, nor can I eat bread or
drink water with you in this place. 17 I have
been told by the word of the Lord: 'You must
not eat bread or drink water there or return
by the way you came.'"*

*18 The old prophet answered, "I too am a
prophet, as you are. And an angel said to me
by the word of the Lord: 'Bring him back
with you to your house so that he may eat
bread and drink water.'" (But he was lying
to him.) 19 So the man of God returned with
him and ate and drank in his house.*

*20 While they were sitting at the table, the
word of the Lord came to the old prophet
who had brought him back. 21 He cried out
to the man of God who had come from
Judah, "This is what the Lord says: 'You
have defied the word of the Lord and have
not kept the command the Lord your God*

gave you. 22 You came back and ate bread and drank water in the place where he told you not to eat or drink. Therefore your body will not be buried in the tomb of your ancestors.'"

23 When the man of God had finished eating and drinking, the prophet who had brought him back saddled his donkey for him. 24 As he went on his way, a lion met him on the road and killed him, and his body was left lying on the road, with both the donkey and the lion standing beside it.

The young prophet did not get sick but the result of his action was death. As I type, I can see many tables with food on it. I can also see the preparers of these dishes. Though all of the dishes on each table looks appealing, not all of the food presented is healthy for one's growth. Besides the food, my attention is on the one who prepared the food. As I look in the spirit, I can see the spirit of some of these preparers is not right. What they have done is learned how to present what people like in order that they may trap them. What does that sound like? Charisma right? If we look closely at these verses, we can see that there are two people revealed in the older prophet. You will see the flesh man and then you can see the spiritual man. The flesh man was full of jealousy. The 11th verse reveals that: "Now there was a certain old prophet living in Bethel." My understanding of this verse is that the young prophet had come in town with a command from the Lord, a fresh word from the Lord concerning what was happening in that region and lastly demonstration that God was indeed with Him. The old prophet could have been set in his ways and when he heard that a young new prophet was in town getting all of the action, he may have gotten jealous. Remember how the old prophet's sons had come back heralding the praises of what a great work that the young prophet was doing. This jealousy moved the old prophet into manipulation and great deceit. However, we see that before the young prophet had gotten to the old prophet how God gave him a command to follow which went like this: "you must not eat bread or drink water there or return by the way you came." This command was given because God sees all things and knew that the young prophet would encounter much deceit. As a prophet, anytime that you are sent on a journey with a word and assignment from the Lord, the enemy will look for a way to destroy your very life in order that you do not become the fulfilment of that very assignment. The purpose of the attack is to stop your heavenly assignment. Anything remotely that reflects God and is working for the betterment of God's kingdom in the earth, the devil is coming after. However, just like the young prophet, the Lord will store us up with a word that will become weapons for us to refer to in order to win every spiritual battle. However, we will have to do what the Word of God says which is to be strong in the Lord and in the power of His might that we are able to stand against the wiles of the enemy. That old prophet was set in his old ways and when he heard of the news that bore witness to the successful ministry of a new young prophet, he got jealous and allowed for another spirit to enter him and use him to stop a work that he should have been working alongside the young prophet.

The other side of the old prophet was the spiritual side. It is funny because it was not until after the old prophet was used of the devil to give false words and the young prophet obeyed it that the old prophet really received a true word from the Lord. Verse 20, "While they were sitting at the table, the word of the Lord came to the old prophet who had brought him back." This is where discernment comes in; we must know and agree with the fact that just because a person has a title does not mean that we should totally drop our arms (stop praying, hearing God for ourselves, etc). We have to be aware of their flesh side as well as their spiritual side. In the event you just cannot discern what side you are in communication with, just obey the last word God told you. This would have kept that young prophet from dying out of season.

There are three things that you can do that will result in your spiritual death:

1. Disobeying God's command

We were not created to engage in wickedness. 1 Samuel 15:23: "For rebellion is as the sin of witchcraft, and stubbornness is as iniquity and idolatry. Because you have rejected the word of the LORD, he has also rejected you from being king." Whenever the Lord gives a command it is for our own spiritual protection. We are in this flesh and of course the enemy wants us to defy anything that aligns with the will of God for our lives. This is why we must choose to walk according to the spirit and not the flesh, so that when the commandment of the Lord comes, our spirit man will be more receptive and dominant over our flesh. The spirit seeks to walk in agreement with the words of God while the flesh works to cancel it out. We must walk in God in order that we might obey him. After all, obedience is the key to growth with God and your earthly assignment.

2. Having loyalty to men with titles

This is an area where many people have the most difficult time. This is the place where they do not have a problem hearing God, but wrestle with whether or not they will receive support from their current covering. While we appreciate and honor God for giving shepherds after His own heart, we must come into the truth of knowing that God is our ultimate covering. Many have heard God to launch into something new and amazing but have decided to reject it on behalf of "receiving Godly counsel" from their mentors or Pastors. It is my belief that true spiritual counsel should not be seeking to rob one of the opportunities of flourishing into their unique callings but rather encouragement and confirmation on whatever God has said. Prophets are feelers which means that they can feel the spirit in which the counsel is flowing. People must realize that obedience to God will sometimes breed a breach between the counselor and counselee. On the flip side obedience to man will most definitely breed a breach between God and the counselee. We should fear God rather than man. Obey God Saints!

3. Dining in a forbidden place

As developing Christians, we grow in relationship with the Holy Spirit. There are certain spiritual tables that we absolutely have no business dining. There are many anointings that linger in the spirit realm. We do not need everyone's approval or anointing collaboration in order to be a success in God. All you need is the one whom the Lord has divinely placed you under. When we eat at too many tables it causes one to move into confusion about what they really should be doing in their earthy call. This is dangerous because it could put you on a path that is not the correct path for your life, even though, you receive man's applause. Check the tables you choose to dine at saints and if it be of the Lord's will for your life.

Prayer:

Father, in the name of Jesus, I thank you for another time of fellowship with you. I thank you that you have reminded us that we are a precious people called by you to do mighty and effective works in the earth. Father we call to remembrance your word found in 1 Peter 2:9-10, "But you are a chosen race, a royal priesthood, a holy nation, a people for his own possession, that you may proclaim the excellencies of him who called you out of darkness into his marvelous light. 10 Once you were not a people, but now you are God's people; once you had not received mercy, but now you have received mercy." We thank you for calling us to be cautious and aware of the tables that we dine. We thank you for making us precious and chosen for a people in our now and future. Father for every spirit of deception that presents itself as an angel of light you will cause us to discern and not be entrapped with its evil desire. In Jesus' mighty name. Amen

Chapter 16

The Gift of Quiet Seasons

Mark 1:35 Expanded Bible (EXB):

35 [Very] Early the next morning, while it was still dark, Jesus ·woke [got up] and left the house. He went to a ·lonely [isolated; deserted] place, where he prayed.

Jesus being the messiah and the talk of the town because of many notable miracles, understood the importance of having moments of peace and quiet with God. When you are called to the high places with God it will attract both good and evil.

Matthew 4:23 (NIV)

"Jesus went throughout Galilee, teaching in their synagogues, proclaiming the good news of the kingdom, and healing every disease and sickness among the people."

The people came because Jesus had a Word in His mouth that would bring forth definite change in their lives. People came looking for a word that worked. Let us look at the strength of this text and see that the people that would be drawn to Jesus were mainly those that had issues and problems. This

Scripture teaches us that as a result of Jesus' Word proclamations and teachings, the demonstration of the power of God showed up. In other words, the validation that Jesus had heard from God and was using the Word correctly, proved to His advantage in the manifestation of healings. Surely this caliber of ministry could not be walked by a person who did not spend quiet times with God. It is my belief that when we spend quiet times with God, we are able to meditate on God and God alone. This mediation is essential because it takes your mind on a journey into the very essence of who God is. Meditation navigates us into the understanding of God's will for our lives. It is my belief that many seek to operate in God without spending quality time with Him. I can testify that in my youth I would pray but not really labor in prayer. I would go out expecting to have access to God's full power. I was dedicated to praying but did not know so much about plowing in the spirit until al little later in my youth. There is a difference between praying and laboring. Praying is communication with God. The purpose is to express yourself and wait on his thoughts. Laboring is when you linger in the presence of the Lord. This lingering is so that you can receive a divine impartation from the Lord. This is where the wailing and travailing takes place. However, little did I know that we only get access into the spirit to the measurement of our labor in the spirit. Much prayer, much power. Moderate prayer, moderate power. Little prayer, little power is all true. So again, I say, there is a huge difference between praying and laboring in prayer. I was talking to a Pastor and he took me to a Scripture in Colossians and reminded me that if one is to become a constant in flowing in the depth of who God is, that person would need to operate out of the revelation of God. We can only get this by spending quiet time with him and laboring in the spirit.

Colossians 1:9-10

9 For this cause we also, since the day we heard it, do not cease to pray for you, and to desire that ye might be filled with the knowledge of his will in all wisdom and spiritual understanding; 10 That ye might walk worthy of the Lord unto all pleasing, being fruitful in every good work, and increasing in the knowledge of God;

You see how there is a great and mighty benefit to having quiet time with God. It is during this time that we can be filled with greater wisdom and revelation from God for the purpose of carrying out His will in the earth. We have got to see ourselves as vehicles of God. We have got to see ourselves as people that have been anointed by God to be a vessel for his glory to fill the earth. If we do not spend quality time with God, then we will not know what he is saying about us and about his people. We will then become incapable of releasing the mysteries of God into the earth and pouring into the people the greatness of our Lord.

Ephesians 1:7

That the God of our Lord Jesus Christ, the Father of glory, may give unto you the spirit of wisdom and revelation in the knowledge of him:

The Apostle Paul is praying and laboring in his quiet time for the church of Ephesus. His deep and sincere desire is to see this church move and function in its highest capacity with God. This is a part of why you must pray Pastor. You must labor Apostle/Prophet. It is so that you can begin to start praying for the church to have what it cannot discern it was destined to have and to operate in. This church of Ephesus was too busy attacking Pastors that came to serve their community with the truth of God's word. Paul had to step in to pray that this church would receive the keys of the spirit and to discern when God had sent a true gift among them.

Prayer:

Father thank you for quiet seasons. Seasons that are so needed. Seasons where you will lead one to pray for themselves yet to labor on behalf of the church. We are open to receive the riches of your word. To be used to declare these wonderful truths to your people. Father, help us to give ourselves fully over to you. Yes, to get back into spending quiet times of meditation with you. Father, be the navigation system of our spirits again. Help us to undergird one another again. Help us to be empowered with a deep longing and desire for spending time with you again. Drive out every distraction. Distract my distractions. Help me to bring my mind in when I'm laboring with you in the spirit. Father I thank you. In Jesus' name. Amen.

Chapter 17

Vine and Vinedresser

John 15:1

I am the true vine, and My Father is the vinedresser.

Dr. Earl Radmacher once asked the question, "What is Jesus saying with the imagery of the "vine" and "vinedresser"? Who are the vine and the vinedresser? I can remember a dream whereby which I heard this Scripture in my spiritual hearing. The Scripture says he that has an ear let him hear what the spirit is saying unto the churches. I wondered what message God was trying to deliver over into my spirit. At the time of the dream, I was wrestling with some decisions that would either bless my purpose or potentially crush my purpose. I was surely in the valley of decision. Whatever choice I made had to be the right one in order for me to reap the benefits of what God had in store for my life. I feel deeply in my heart at this moment that there are many of you that are struggling with making the right decisions. I feel impressed by the spirit to tell you to remember who you are and then reminisce on who God is. You don't know the course of your life except by the spirit. You are going to have to get in the spirit before making any moves with your life. Yes, it a very awkward season of your life. Trust God with your life. Press into Him to help you make your decisions. Doing this will determine the kind of harvest or fruit that is manifested in your future. Trust God and not what you see or hear. Trust the God of your spirit.

Job 12:10

"and that the life of every living thing rests in his control, along with the breath of every living human being?"

The prophet Isaiah reminds us in the 49th chapter that our names are inscribed in the palms of God's hands. Note that our names are not on just one palm but on both palms of God's hands. This is assurance to us that we are forever upon the mind of God and that He cannot forget who we are. God knows who we are and what we were created for. We do not have time to allow access to the enemy of our soul to infiltrate our minds with ambiguity or uncertainty about why we live. Job offers us further hope that in God's hand is our very life and our breath. We have to live this life with confidence knowing that we belong in the era that we were born. It is imperative that we understand that God is in control of our destiny.

Well, let us examine the words given by the spirit of God to John in the 15th chapter and the first verse:

I am the true vine, and My Father is the vinedresser.

Just like a shepherd is acquainted with his sheep so is a vinedresser his vines. Jesus speaks to his disciples in such a way in order to make them aware that they are not in control, but that God is at the seat of their lives. Jesus uses his own life as a perfect example of what the relationship between the father and the one who trusts him should look like. Jesus exemplifies that he is well provided for in every way. He essentially points to the truth that God has not brought him to earth just to leave him in lack. As a matter of fact, the relationship between he and the father is the heartbeat of his existence on earth. When everything would seemingly go wrong and there seemed to be no earthly hope, his connection with God was the lifeline in the midst of trouble. Jesus uses this scripture as imagery to show that when we are connected to God, we can be confident and rest assured that we are safe. We can rest assured that we are in good company and therefore look for growth and productivity. Jesus moved further with essentially exposing that a part of this growth process involves a cut.

John 15:2

He cuts off every branch in me that bears no fruit, while every branch that does bear fruit he prunes so that it will be even more fruitful.

In order to grow we cannot be so naïve to think that we do not have things attached to our lives that need to be abraised. Notice that Jesus said that there was a lack of productivity because of what was inwardly. A lot of people are suffering growth problems and their mentality of the growth dysfunction is backwards. They are fighting non- existing demonic external forces. They think that the reasoning behind their lack, failure, unproductivity and lack of growth is tied to some opposing force on the external.

In some instances this can be true;however, in this 2nd verse of John 15, Jesus shows 2 powerful truths for the relationship between God and his own:

1. The Vinedresser cuts off inward hindrances

This cutting away is not of the devil but is God's will. In fact, the devil would love this lack of fruit bearing to remain in you so that you will be stuck. It is the enemy's desire that we are blinded to the things in us that is causing our growth to be stunted. He does not want pride, low confidence, perversion, arrogance, etc... to be detected in our spirit because these are the kinds of things that will cause growth retardation. But the Vinedresser shows up to attack the lack in our lives. He steps on the scene of our lives to come after everything in us that is causing us not to be the very best that we have the potential of being. This is also an opportunity for the Lord to mature us with knowing every hinderance is not external, but it is possible that it is internal. This is the season that we get the truth about ourselves. The truth is the thing that will set us free and release us into the deeper things of the spirit. You can always tell a person that has come through a cutting season by how well they are flourishing in the things of the spirit. They are not hindered in any way.

2. The Vinedresser prunes that which is producing

This, in my opinion, is one of the most difficult seasons of a born-again believer. This is the season where you are flourishing, moving forward in ministry and suddenly God tells you to stop. You are in what seems like the prime of your ministry and now you are counseled by the Lord to stop. What you thought was ok, God wants to make better. This is the season that helps to keep the believer from being lifted in pride. This is the season where they get to see that though they are producing there is yet another level in them that God is wanting to help bring them to. This minister would need to be willing and open to the pruning process. They will need not think that just because they have "stuff", as result of their ministering, that they can not become better. This kind of attitude will not be acceptable with this stage of the perfection process.

Prayer:

Father in Jesus' name, I thank you for healing my perspective to know that I have room for growth. I thank you God that though you have allowed space for me to celebrate what has already been,you, father will not leave me on a stale and exhausted level. I thank you that you will only bring challenge to the one that you seek to pour greater into. Help me to lay aside pride and to follow your plan and your will for my life. The cutting may hurt. It might even leave a great scar. Father I know that those that have done mighty exploits in you have had great scars. So, help us to suck it up and be grateful for the opportunity to grow greater than ever before. In Jesus' name, Amen.

Chapter 18

Relationship Discernment

There are two kinds of people that will grace your life: seasonal friends and eternal friends. Seasonal friends are people that come into your life for a brief moment. Eternal friends are those that come into your life and it will be as it is with marriage vows,"until death do us part." Having seasonal friends is no less of value than having eternal friendships. I believe that there are people that God will divinely send into your life for a seasonal impartation. This seasonal impartation can be for you towards the person, the person towards you or vice versa. As I write, I am reminded of a church that I attended. I had come to the ministry after a bad experience. However, before I had decided to be a part of this fellowship, God had been dealing with me on relocating. I did not want to leave the city. I wanted to stay and just be a ministry gift. As a child, I have always asked the Lord to use me. I have always had a burning desire to help people in whatever capacity they needed. When I joined this ministry I made it known in the beginning that I was only going to be in the city for a short time. Though I knew this, I still wanted to work while there. The Pastor of this ministry was very sensitive and keen on who God was calling me to be and what he was calling me to do. He allowed me to come into his ministry and to serve. There were several vacancies and I knew that I could be of help for the duration of time I would be there. I thoroughly enjoyed myself at this ministry. I enjoyed the preaching ministry of the Pastor as the word would always be sufficient for my soul. Being up under that word was what helped me to stay afloat until my departure. We were able to help one another. I was able to come in and sow my talents into the ministry and the Pastor allowed for me to have a place of refuge and strength while I was still in the city. However, this is an example of a seasonal ministry relationship. Was this a bad connection? Absolutely not. To this day we are still in contact. Nonetheless, God will help you to define and properly categorize people that come into your life.

Many people have become hurt unnecessarily because when someone came into their life, they grew too attached to them too quickly. They immediately labeled them as eternal when indeed they were only to be a part of their lives for a season. You have to be careful with this. To not properly discern a person's role in your life and how long they are to be there will get you in trouble. You will start making all of these plans for their life and putting assignments on them that may distract them from their God purpose. Pastors have to especially watch this because if not careful they will give someone an assignment that might take a person 10 years to complete with excellence. The problem with this is that God may shift that person after 4 years. If pastors are not cautious, they will move out of the spirit and into the flesh and start wrongfully bashing the very person they said was God sent. Pastors must be sure to receive flock without an agenda. They must be careful of the things that they say about their flock to other flock and to other leaders in that city. It does not matter if what is said is not true, because of the position that the pastor hold and the influence that he or she has on others, people will listen. Due to this dilemma, the innocent person will have to start fighting against all of the false judgment spoken against their integrity and character. This will all be because the pastor lacked discernment of that person's part in their lives and because they are in the flesh. People who do damage in the heat of their emotions will find it difficult to fully rectify the person's reputation that they were responsible for damaging.

Healing is what many need-from the choir stand to the pulpit to the pew. The house of God is in need of deep healing. The way we gossip about one another, hate on one another, wish harm on one another etc.. is outrageous. This only stems from vessels that have been hurt and that have not been healed. Can anything broken and tattered be a source of pure love and compassionate care? Let's pause here.. I will let you answer that!

Some ways to discern whether or not a person is to be seasonal or eternal in your lifeare as follows:

A. Seasonal relationships

a) God will tell you that the connection is temporary

b) Though concerned about a person, you won't feel a deep spiritual connection

c) You won't feel sad if they decide to exit your life

d) You won't feel the need to invest deeply into the connection

B. Eternal relationship

a) God will tell you that the connection is eternal

b) You will feel a special desire to have this person in your life even though you may not discern the reason in the beginning

c) You will feel as if there is a deep sadness if they decide to leave your life

d) You will discern by the spirit that you should invest your time, effort and energy into this connection.

I feel led to encourage someone that whether you have seasonal or eternal relationships, they all have meaning. I feel led to testify in this moment. From a child on into my adult life I have had more seemingly seasonal relationships than eternal. This left me feeling as though something was wrong with me. As I began to grow, I realized how it did not matter how long a person stayed in my life, they all had one thing in common. This common thing was that they all would express how genuine their interactions with me had been a blessing in their lives. This made me realize that sometimes God will bring people by your way to lift up their spirits to know that there is hope. Now, when I meet people I do not immediately attach. Instead, I ask God who they are and why we met. This helps me to have balance and to know how far to go with the person. You have to know that you are special and that God knows what he is doing. Love the eternal people that he has graced to be a part of your life. Embrace those who are seasonal. And when it's time to let them go, release them in love and without bashing them. Identify who they are in the beginning and you will have a smooth ending with them.

Prayer:

Father, in the name of Jesus, I thank you once again for allowing me another chance to express my love and thanks towards you. Father, relationships are beautiful. In the beginning you created humans to be relational. For this we tell you thank you. Father we ask that as we move along in this life that you would cause us to properly identify the people that come into our lives. Help us to see them as long term or short term relationships. If they are long term, father help us to give 100 percent focus into building a good connection. Help me to honor, accept and cherish my friend. Help me to give what I have been assigned to give them as well as to receive what I am called to receive from them. Father for those that have been assigned to my life for a short while, help me to embrace them and love them. Cause us to accomplish the purpose of the short term connection. Father, when it's time for us to part, help us to depart with thanksgiving in our hearts. Cause us to pronounce blessings upon one another. Let this be our words: may the Lord watch in between me and thee. While we are absent one from another in Jesus' name, Amen.

Chapter 19

Fulfillment

Psalm 16:11 English Standard Version (ESV)

You make known to me the path of life; in your presence there is fullness of joy; at your right hand are pleasures forevermore.

You can flow in the prophetic and still feel incomplete. I believe that this is because God wants you to know that your satisfaction is not in the prophet, prophecy or thing manifested. Rather your fulfillment is in God alone. I believe that God orchestrates it to be this way because He wants us in that insatiable place. To be in an insatiable place simply means to be in a place where our hunger never ends. I believe that this is the place where the Lord wants us to be while pursuing after him. This is the place where God can constantly fill us. Every day the Lord is looking for ways to load us with benefits.

Psalms 68:19

"19 Blessed be the Lord, who daily loadeth us with benefits, even the God of our salvation. Selah."

It is the place that while we are grateful to him for supplying for us, we realize that one time impartation is not enough to keep us for the remainder of our journey. It's like a car that stops at the filling station to get filled with gas to drive a certain distance. Once that car reaches that distance, it is usually time for another filling. God will manifest his promises and the excitement will only last but for a moment before we find ourselves reaching for him, because the time for re-filling has come. I was searching the Scriptures found in Luke 4. It was while reading this chapter that I heard the Lord say, "You must reach the insatiable place." Let's take a look at the verses:

Luke 4: 1-2:

1 "Jesus, full of the Holy Spirit, left the Jordan and was led by the Spirit into the wilderness, 2 where for forty days he was tempted[a] by the devil. He ate nothing during those days, and at the end of them he was hungry."

We can clearly see how before we decide to do anything it is important for us to be full of the Holy Spirit. While reading this Scripture I learned that immediately after the filling of the Holy Spirit came a level of warfare that could only be won with the assistance of the Holy Spirit. Jesus had not eaten anything of the natural which shows us that he really was not relying on anything of natural means for strength. Jesus understood that eating bread and drinking a little water would have given him strength in his physical body but it would have been too weak to give him victory over the satanic attack at hand. Instead, Jesus leaned upon God for strength. His absence from natural food was essentially a message to say that real victory is not in bread and water but in God and God alone. Fasting is a direct sign that one's reliance is upon God and his mighty hand. However, I want to look at something else in this verse. After the warfare had ended with the devil, the bible says that Jesus afterward hungered. The question that stood out to me was why did Jesus hunger? I know you must be saying sis it states why...it was because he had just come off of a 40 day fast without bread and water. Jesus was ready to eat hunny. Lol. To the natural mind that would make perfect sense. However, my thoughts were aligned more along the lines that while Jesus was thankful for the victory won in the last season of warfare, he still had an inner hunger within that would keep him on a search after God. Jesus knew that the devil would be persistent. If we look at verses 3-11, it reveals how the warfare would be geared towards one's self identity. The devil kept posing questions that started with, 'if you are.....'' These kinds of questions are laced with great deception to manipulate one's mind into a realm of confusion about who they are in God. I believe that when Jesus was hungry he had entered that insatiable place. It is in this insatiable place that we remain in a posture of prayer and holiness as we know that these are the things that grab God's attention to look upon us and our situations with favor.

Though God had delivered Jesus out of the fiery tempting trial of the devil, he had to keep Jesus hungering after him so that he would continue winning the battle. Often times we want to rest after victories. There is nothing wrong with pausing to celebrate your triumphs but please do not pitch your tents and later build your house there. Every time you win a battle you make Satan more divisive towards you. Why? Let's look at verse 13 in Luke 4.

13 When the devil had finished all this tempting, he left him until an opportune time.

Wow! Do you see what I see? Well let me help you just in case you don't... The devil was coming back to tempt Jesus. Jesus had to remain with a hunger so that every time the devil would show up in his life he would never find an open invitation because Jesus was always in the presence of the Lord being filled up by God. You see beloved, the devil will come and go out of your life. Have you ever experienced heavy seasons of temptation with some kind of sin? I know I have. These seasons are inevitable. The devil will be the devil. It is his job to roam and to seek whom he may devour.

Let me pause here. I feel led to expose something. Your temptation does not mean that you are sinful. It only reveals what's in your sinful nature. It is what you do with these temptations that push you into the category of being a blatant sinner. I need you to know that the devil picks up on your curiosities through your conversations. Often times we talk about what makes us curious. However, it does not matter what you are being tempted with, it does not have more power over your decisions about it. You have the power to decide the fate of what's tempting you. Just as adamant as the devil is to devour our vessels we have got to be just as adamant to keep our vessels swept, cleaned and filled up. In doing this, it will not matter which season the enemy shows up to tempt us because we will always be filled up.

We know that reading God's word, praying, and consecrating ourselves unto the Lord are all great ways to becoming strong in our spirit man. Let us examine another powerful step to consider while striving to defeat the enemy:

Conversation with your leader or mentor-talking is a great way to expose the enemy. In this step you are able to express in detail how the enemy has been taunting your mind and soul over certain issues in this life. Indeed the Scriptures declare how we will have many tribulations. However, it also reveals how we will have deliverance out of them all. When we are in conversation with someone of strong discernment and wisdom, it puts us at an advantage. This advantage causes us to receive insights that we were previously blinded to because of the great warfare towards us. Talking about your temptation can also help the mentor pinpoint how they can best pray for you while going through your season of tempting.

Prayer:

Father in Jesus' name, I thank you that you have made known to us a part of your will for our lives is that we be filled with you in every season of our lives. I thank you that when you look upon me you have victory in mind for my life. I ask now God that you will cause me to live in the insatiable place. Yes Lord, that place described in Psalms 91:1 as described as the secret place. Yes, Lord Help me to be like Jesus Christ in that after I have reached this place that I will have the discipline to fulfill the rest of the verse of Psalms 91:1, in that I will abide there. Help me to always be reminded that my victory is not in bread and water, but my victory is always found in that insatiable place in you. It is here that I will forever be made prepared to face whatever temptations Satan has planned for my life. Amen. #Iwin

Chapter 20

How Well He Knows Us

Psalms 139:1

"You have looked deep into my heart, LORD, and you know all about me."

There is not one thing that concerns you that God does not see. As I write I am reminded how as a young girl I would try to hide my emotions from my mother. To this day I cannot tell you why I felt that I was smart enough to attempt this. It did not matter how many smiles I put on my face or kind words I gave others, my mother would always see right through me. Oh how I hated this. I am the kind of person that does not like to burden others with my issues. My mother has always had a way of using her sweet and caring ways to help me through my rough moments. This is how God does us. We live in this very cruel and, at times, vicious world where we are constantly under attack. We try to appear tough but deep down inside we will have to admit that we are fragile and damaged from the constant abruptions. People can tell when you are hurt because most people will suddenly change their attitudes, dispositions and their tolerance levels won't be as long as normal. It is in moments like these that we must be honest enough with ourselves to take a reprieve or a break from dealing with certain people and certain situations. I believe this happens because we put more on ourselves than we can handle.

God knows us and just how much we can handle.

1 Corinthians 10:13,

"No temptation [regardless of its source] has overtaken or enticed you that is not common to human experience [nor is any temptation unusual or beyond human resistance]; but God is faithful [to His word—He is compassionate and trustworthy], and He will not let you be tempted beyond your ability [to resist], but along with the temptation He [has in the past and is now and] will [always] provide the way out as well, so that you will be able to endure it [without yielding, and will overcome temptation with joy]."

He knows everything about who we are even when we don't have the full concept of ourselves. God uses just the right amount of pressure to reveal to us the level of strength that we possess. This is why it is important that we take the necessary time to spend quality time with the Lord.

There are 2 things that can damage us; spending too much time with people who do not see you by the spirit and not studying once your purpose is revealed. It is critical that we are cautious of who we lend our ears to when walking in the infancy of our God assignments. If we allow the wrong person into our space while we are striving towards completion it could delay us. You must decide that you are valuable. You must determine that. After you have determined your value, you must decide not to eliminate anything out of your life that looks like anything that is beneath that. Never allow people, life or your own doubts to lower the standard that God set for your life. I heard the Lord say that you must connect with people that are on the next level of your potential. If you want to get to the next level you must decide that you are worth investing into and that your circle must look like your future and not your past or present condition. The next thing you have to do is invest in books that can feed you knowledge

about how to become a success in the area
that God has called you into. the anointing
alone will not cut it. Prayer alone will not
work. Reading the Scriptures alone will not
work. You are going to have to make up in
your mind that you are going to invest into
your future via conferences, mentorship or
secular books. Say Glory! lol

Chapter 21

Send Someone Else

Exodus 4:13, "But he said, "Oh, my Lord, please send someone else.""

Often times we give excuses for the assignment that we were chosen by God to do. Some of the most common ones sound like this:

- God, but they don't like me

- God, I don't have the fan base

- God, I don't have the degree

- God, I don't have good social skills

- God, no one in my family has ever accomplished that

- God, I may fail

- God, I lack confidence

- God, my thoughts are not established

- God people always drop me

- God I struggle with belief in my own calling

These are just a surface of excuses that mankind have given God on account of them not being able to achieve their purpose. However, as I was driving to work the Lord began to share with me a valuable piece of information. My thoughts were aligned along the truth that before we accomplished anything in this life, God had already chosen us for the kingdom assignment at hand. One reason why I believe that King Solomon warned us from looking to the left and to the right was to keep us from being disturbed or discouraged to move forward in destiny based upon what others had. In these moments we are desiring to have what took someone over 20 years to accomplish. You see it's like with the prophets Elijah and Elisha and the anointing and calling on their lives. You see, we get geeked because we read that the scripture reveals how Elisha walked in double of what Elijah had. However, we must know that in order for Elisha to have walked in double blessings, Elisha would have also had to walk in double warfare. You don't think that the devil would let you just rise up and be a great asset in the earth without fighting you, do you? The fight is a demonic force sent from hell to drain you of all your strength.

This strategy is so that you will stop being the blessing that you are to mankind. It is sent to stop kingdom movement. However, I also want to say that the dangers of measuring yourself with others will ultimately result in vision abandonment. The apostle Paul wrote a potent piece found in 1 Corinthians 16:9, "for a wide door for effective work has opened to me, and there are many adversaries." The Apostle Paul is such an inspiration to many. Though short in stature, he was a giant in faith and fundamentals. When Paul was converted he did not adopt a spirit of timidity or slack. This apostle was just as tenacious as he was when a devout Pharisee. Paul wanted to reach as many people as he could with the gospel of Jesus Christ. His main focal point was winning souls. I feel lead to prophesy that this is where we are on God's agenda. God is restoring the agenda for ministry again. God is redirecting our attention back on serving him to win souls. I declare that we will evangelize to win souls. We will prophesy to win souls. We will teach to win souls. We will move forward in whatever facet of ministry we're called to in order to win souls. May souls be our agenda again. May we trust the Scripture that says if we seek the kingdom of God (spiritual) that all other things (natural needs for effective ministry) will be given. I prophesy that as you are making up your mind to start God's work, God is awakening your destiny helper to assist you with purpose.

But let's really look at what Paul was saying in Corinthians 16:9. I am sure that the apostle Paul was excited to have more opportunities to go into unfamiliar territory for the sole purpose of establishing governmental orders and winning souls for the kingdom of God. However, another adjective to describe Paul is warrior. Though the doors were opening for him, they did not come with ease or without a fight. I am laughing at this moment because I can hear in my spirit that war only comes to do two things:

1. **To make you a warrior**

2. **Activate warlike abilities**

In other words, anyone that answers the call to walk into effective doors will need to prepare to enter into war zones.

The doors that will open for you are only going to be as wide as the degree of your education and preparation for the reality of demonic darts that will be thrown your way. You see, the devil doesn't mind that you walk through doors just as long as you are blinded to the traps and setups meant for your failure. I can hear someone in my spirit right now saying, "Well how can it be possible to make it through a door of success and then fail at your assignment?" Well, I'm glad you asked beloved.

I had a dream and I saw how a wide and effective door had been opened for me. I saw myself in the company of giants in the kingdom. However, I saw my facial expression in a nearby view, which was a look of stress and agitation. I also felt uneasy. I began to ask God why. In a time where I should have been excited and rejoicing, I wasn't. I then began to look around and I saw faces of familiar people who I had taken with me whose spirit had changed and wasn't right towards me. They were purposely doing things that they knew would bother me. I was there in that atmosphere to participate on program but just couldn't gather my thoughts. I then began to develop a negative attitude and started trying to get them back. It was then that I heard, "No, do you not see their plot. They are doing these things to cause you to come out of character before those who admire you. You can not afford to do so." I woke up.

Please dear people, allow me to enlighten you in this moment. I saw several things in that dream.

1. **Effective door opened**
2. **Great opponents**
3. **Demonic afflictions**
4. **Negative attitude development**

You see if you don't ask God to show you how to handle people and their agendas, it can cause you to mess up the good thing that God has in store for you. It's sad how one response could cause a door filled with so many possibilities to shut, all because you didn't prepare for your warfare. I don't care where you go and who you deal with, you will find that people really are the same.

You have to ask God to teach you how to respond to oppositions that arise. You won't have the luxury to respond back with how they treat you. Let me enlighten you on what you should be asking God to help you with and even possibly studying through books.

1. How to release all inner agitations and to walk in a peace that surpasses all understanding
2. How to deal with people in general
3. How to maintain a healthy outlook or attitude
4. How to choose your battles; everything is not worth your response
5. How to see the true spirit of man and yet work with him to get a kingdom job done. Don't quit every time you see something ungodly in a person. Remember how the woman who served Jesus was not a Christian. However, she helped to prepare him for destiny. STOP RUNNING!
6. How to choose your team- sometimes it includes a Judas
7. How to not give attention to low "truths"
8. How to handle warfare coming from a relative

9. How to remain focused on what's important and please God in every season
10. How to appreciate and honor the ones who truly stand with you.

Prayer: Father, you are the one who opens and closes doors. God I ask that you help me to mature beyond my chronological years and to soar into the wisdom of my ancestors. God in my youth and middle age I ask for wisdom. Grant me the ability to deal with myself and people. Help me to not miss the blessing that you've prepared for my life on account of my untamed tongue. I thank you in advance. In Jesus name, Amen.

Chapter 22

Man's Disappointment, God's Appointment

It's a known fact that people develop in their thoughts who you should blossom into. Some people may envision you to be a famous preacher. Some may envision you to be an athlete. Some people may have envisioned you to become a professor at a prestigious university. Maybe some envisioned you to be a millionaire or some great author. Whatever they envisioned was for their benefit. When people desire for you to become something, often times, it is for their pleasure. I have seen this especially in the church arena. I have seen where pastors would groom members with an agenda in mind. They would boost these people up and give them "high" positions in the church. Someone called me to express their deep disgruntled spirit about what they had gone through in their church. They expressed that as long as they were going along with that pastor's plan they were being praised and loved. However, they expressed that as they started challenging their leader on some of the things asked to be done, things started to get a little rocky. The pastor would use the pulpit to impute their ill feelings on this individual. The Pastor started asking other members to go over the work of the one who was supposedly the awesome "person" of God. The pastor started to disclose the personal information of this person to other members in the house causing those members to have a faulty vision of this person. The pastor would act dumbfounded when this person approached them to explain how 40% of the church knew what they had only disclosed with them. All of this happened only because the pastor could not control the outcome of this person. The person was starting to disappoint this pastor by moving at the beat of God's drum and as a result, the pastor tried to kill this person's character. In this moment the pastor was viewing the member as a disappointment. I want to encourage someone not to allow such treatment to keep you stuck. Joseph said, "They meant it for my bad, but God turned it around for my good." In other words what Joseph was saying was that they did this for the purposes of causing me to feel inadequate or inferior. However, God would use the same situation as a means to develop Joseph and make him well experienced and capable. Joseph may have been viewed as a major disappointment to his brothers and even his Father, but he was right on schedule for the appointment of destiny. I want to help someone here, in that often when you decide to obey God's orders, you will be viewed as a rebel or disappointment. Sometimes the disappointment with man can be used as a prophetic sign that you are moving in the right direction and are about to become what God had already appointed and predestined for you to evolve into.

Prayer: Father, I know that your thoughts about me are good however; they can at times breed contempt with my contemporaries. Today I ask that you will free me from the pressure of man's approval yet being disapproved by you. Cause me in every season of my life to hold your expectations of me higher than what man desires of my life. Keep me mentally healthy though the stones are thrown only on the basis that I choose you and not popularity or mans' claps. Help me to forever walk in your truth about me. I believe therefore I will "be." Amen.

Chapter 23

Soar

Isaiah 40:31:

But those who hope in the LORD will renew their strength. They will soar on wings like eagles; they will run and not grow weary, they will walk and not be faint.

I prophesy that you will not live your life suppressed under the opinions of your contemporaries. Be free of the negative words that was laced with a demonic assignment to damage your perception. I prophesy that your conceptualization of yourself will be healthy and in alignment with what God sees about you. You will only pursue your God assignments in the earth and will not fall prey to pursuing an image or career based upon what others suggest about your life. You will soar. You will soar because you will release people of their power over you. You are stripping the enemy of his power over you and people from their influence over you. Your strength is being renewed as you step into the knowledge of your highest calling. God is touching your potential. No longer will you live as everyone else's cheerleader while your purpose goes untouched. In this moment I speak that the Lord is visiting your desires. Yes, the Lord is turning your every desire towards the direction that he has established for your life. I prophesy that you are no longer being drawn to people who see you as a joke. God is strengthening your discernment to discern people's true motives towards you. I prophesy that you will not be pimped in your gifting. I declare that God is going before you to choose your connections. No longer will you entertain a spirit of manipulation and believe that you have to hold on to those who do not have your best interest at heart. I prophesy that you are soaring. You are soaring because you will believe what God reveals about you. Believe Pastor. Believe Evangelist. Believe Prophet. Believe Apostle. Believe servant of God. Believe. I declare that you are soaring. You are soaring because you will focus on your God assignment. Doors are opening as you believe. Ways are being made as you believe. God is preparing opportunities for you as you believe. You will attract wealth. Your relationships are healthy. You are soaring in every area of your life.

3 John 2 King James Version (KJV)

2 Beloved, I wish above all things that thou mayest prosper and be in health, even as thy soul prospereth.

This shall be your portion. Yes, you will become a sign of holistic health. You are soaring.

I want to encourage someone to know that soaring has several dimensions. Though you were born to soar, you will have to go through the steps of development.

- Realize your ability- you cannot become what you do not realize

- Embrace your ability- you must accept that whatever God has revealed about you is what you have been called or chosen by the Lord to do. You must partner with the Lord in order to see your greatness come forth.

- Practice your ability- Look for ways to exercise your ability. If doors do not open for you, create them. Jesus did not cry about people not offering him the opportunity to teach or preach or to perform miracles. He simply tapped into his self-worth and anointed a team and off they went into villages, cities, towns and countries declaring the message on the kingdom of God.

- Stay in the flow- once you are in the flow of your calling do not drop the ball. Dedicate yourself to perfecting the reason why you are in the earth, Be the best Evangelist, CEO, Prophet, Teacher, etc.. that you can be. Be a ministry gift. Study your calling and choose a mentor that you really respect and can count on to be worthy of spending time with.

Prayer:

Father, I thank you that you have called us to soar above the limitations of this world. You have called us out and have made us to be seated in heavenly places in Christ Jesus. Father your word reveals to us that if we decide to hope in you that we will never grow weary or faint. You have called us to soar. You have called us to mount up on wings as eagles. You have not called us to be depressed, suppressed or oppressed. You have spoken your word and breathed life into us and now we can arise and "be". In confidence we go at thy command. We pray like the Apostle Paul and ask for boldness. We declare that we are fearless. We are unstoppable. Father, we thank you that you have made all of this possible. In Jesus' name. Amen

Chapter 24

Planks

Matthew 7:3-5 "Why do you look at the speck of sawdust in your brother's eye and pay no attention to the plank in your own eye? 4 How can you say to your brother, 'Let me take the speck out of your eye,' when all the time there is a plank in your own eye? 5 You hypocrite, first take the plank out of your own eye, and then you will see clearly to remove the speck from your brother's eye."

While listening to a sermon by Dr. Tony Evans he said something that captured my attention, "One thing can be wrong with you but it can ruin the rest of you." What a powerful statement. I decided to dedicate a section on planks do to a dream that I had about them. In the dream, I was looking at a person that was trying to point out everything that was wrong about the other person. This person had a negative spirit as to try to make the other person feel bad about their flaws. However, one part in the dream that amazed me was the fact that what the guy was pointing out about the other person was actually true. This brings me to a point that sometimes when the enemy speaks negative things about us it is the truth. However, it is the motive behind what we say that matters the most. The other thing that was amazing was that the guy also had unresolved issues. However, he could not see them because he was too focused on the flaws of the guy that he was talking about.

The Scripture says that when we are unaware of our own flaws, we are incapable of leading others. We cannot help others overcome when we are still bound up. The Scripture says that they overcame by the blood of the lamb and by the word of their testimony. This speaks volumes because it reveals that if we want to see others overcome, we first must look like deliverance. In the body of Christ there is a lot of fault finding. People are arrogant because they are ignorant of the fact that they have problems that need the blood of Jesus Christ just as much as the person with whom they feel they are superior to. This is another issue in that people have the tendency to feel greater than the next person because they feel as though their sins are not as bad as the next person's. It seems as though people believe that abortion and capital murder is greater than having a lying tongue. However, in the book of James, it states that the tongue is the most dangerous part of the body. What comes out of the mouth carries the potential to kill someone's character or integrity. In Proverbs 6, it reveals how there are 7 abominations and 6 of them God does hate.

Proverbs 6:16-19 King James Version (KJV)

16 These six things doth the Lord hate: yea, seven are an abomination unto him:

17 A proud look, a lying tongue, and hands that shed innocent blood,

18 An heart that deviseth wicked imaginations, feet that be swift in running to mischief,

19 A false witness that speaketh lies, and he that soweth discord among brethren.

Does this mean that these sins are on a higher level than any other sin? There is one sin that is in a category alone. An example of this sin can be found in the story of Esau. When Esau sold his birthright for a bowl of lentils, he committed this sin. The name of this sin is called blasphemy. When we blaspheme against the Holy Spirit, we will find that there will be no reconciliation.

Fornication is not different than lying. Lying is no different than gossiping. Gossiping is no greater than debauchery. Debauchery is no greater than murder. Murder is no greater than stealing. However, if you murdered someone and your friend commits blasphemy, then your friend will be judged at a greater degree.

There is a way that you can become most effective in your approach to help your neighbor to become better. You can work on yourself and become better. When you become better it will put you at an advantage to identify your wrongs as well as to help you identify strategies of becoming better. You can now take your experience and your learned strategies to a generation of people that are struggling with what you have just been delivered from.

Prayer:

Father, in the name of Jesus, I thank you for helping me to see that my planks are a sign that there is an opportunity to grow. I thank you father that you cause me to recognize that I cannot help deliver anyone until I have faced my problems first. I thank you father that it is in my deliverance that you will cause me to receive pertinent understandings to share with others. Father, I thank you that it is because of my frailties that I attract Christ to me and he teaches me to focus on myself. I am healed from my planks with the agenda not to boast upon anything but Christ. Father, I ask that even if I do see the planks of my brothers and sisters that I do not use it as a platform to rise in my confidence, but rather I will see it as an opportunity to pray for them until they are brought to a point of deliverance. Amen.

Chapter 25

Cycles

Deuteronomy 2:3, "Ye have compassed this mountain long enough: turn you northward." (KJV)

Cycles can be defined as repeated motions. It is when someone is going through the same thing repeatedly. It is my belief that this repeated cycle is because of the decisions that a person chooses to make. Sometimes people that are battling with cycles believe that they will in some way receive different results. According to the world system, it is called insanity. However, the Bible identifies it as being blinded:

2 Corinthians 4:4, "The god of this age has blinded the minds of unbelievers." (NIV)

When you are blind it is hard for you to see the truth. You will continue on a path that is an enemy to your true purpose. This will only be because the lie that you've been following has become appealing to you. You have become comfortable with the results that it has produced. Sometimes some results seem better than no results. Some people would rather hold on to the wrong path because it seems like being on the right path was not producing as many results as the old path. I would like to say that sometimes receiving less can be a lot better than receiving much. I would rather get less results and it be what I need in order to get me to my next level than to settle for too much and have to decipher through too much unnecessary ungodly manifestations.

I challenge you today to confess to the Lord and with a trusted friend about your cycles. Tell God how miserable you are and how you need his grace to be delivered. Ask God to reveal to you his true path of victory for your life. Ask your friend to pray with you that you drop your pride so that you can move forward with your life. Understand that though you choose to walk with God on this new path, it may look different than what you expected. Be prepared to walk with few. Get ready to be misunderstood. However, prepare to be freer in your spirit than you've ever been because you have chosen to be true to yourself.

Prayer: Lord, I confess to you that I am stuck. The cycle of religion, pride,

prayerlessness, forms of godliness, etc. are
entangling my very soul. Father, I need your
sense of direction. I thank you for opening
my eyes. I praise you now that the blinders
are falling off of my eyes. I am no longer
trapped by the cycles that impede my life.
I'm free. Yes, I decree that I'm delivered.
Father, I embrace the truth that He whom
the Son sets free is free indeed. I thank you
that with you I can truly say that I am free
from these cycles.

Chapter 26

Locked up Treasures

The Apostle Paul used these words found in the book of Corinthians that there are treasures in these earthen vessels. How amazing enough that the Lord would entrust pearls and great value within dust particles. This is very significant in that deep within the dirtiest of the dirty one would find great value. This is why we can never disregard what looks dull and unattractive. It is my belief that the reason everything begins in its unattractive form first is because it grants the Lord time to perfect it before it is presented to the world for any use. It seems that all things that begin as un-useful ends up being the most talked of or sought after. Let's examine a few things:

1. Caterpillars start off as an ugly cocoon. The cocoon is usually a dirty brown which only draws the attention of negative critics. However, when it blossoms into a beautiful catepillar after being processed, many become mesmerized by how it adds to nature's beauty.

2. Man- Man began as a dust particle. This is the lowest of the lowest. Dirt is what we walk on. It is what we spit on. It is what we trample upon. Yet, the Lord saw deep into it and beyond its abuse that it was enough to form a whole human. This is usually what happens. The Lord uses what is trampled upon and abused and makes something great out of it.

3. World- the World began under water. It was in a dark place. A lonely place. A place that was secluded away from anything else. This is another point in how the Lord will usually call for something that is secluded away from society. I believe this is because it's not tainted or influenced by any other external factors and is in its purest form.

4. Seed- a seed is tiny. It is overlooked. It is forgotten until what's in it is revealed. No one had ever thought of orange seeds until its ability to produce was known.

However, all of these examples could not be as great of use as they are and have been in times past unless pressure was applied upon it.

Pressure can be defined as the necessary applied force needed to produce a product. Without this pressure nothing would exist. The problem with most people is that they want a great product without any pressure. They want to see mighty results without applying the necessary efforts. The truth is that strength is built best by resistance. Without resistance you wouldn't know what does not work. I often say that we have to read our warfare correctly. Resistance can be used as a tool to point you in the direction of your true purpose. There are 2 things that resistance represents and that is:

1. **This is the direction of your purpose**

2. **This is not the direction of your purpose**

There is nothing more satisfying to the devil than for him to see you miss your ultimate destination. According to Romans 1, we were all chosen to be a part of God's glorious plan. When we are on the wrong road we will ultimately miss the path for our lives. The path that we take is in direct correspondance with whether the treasures in us comes out or not. When hard times arise for short or long seasons of your life, don't be discouraged. Oftentimes things get worse before they start getting better. So, I say keep building my brother. Keep striving my sister. Hold your head up high. You can make it. Yes, you will make it through. You may feel pain, but hold on baby, it's just God preparing you to push out that treasure within. Selah.

Chapter 27

Reverence

One night I was led to read Psalms 34 in the Living Bible translation. While reading, there was one word that stood out to me and that word was REVERENCE. I began to see how this one word could give much access to the one that would die to the flesh and exercise it. According to the King James Dictionary, the word reverence is expressed as showing respect or fear. This word reverence carries a different presence in the Old Testament as is in the New Testament. According to the International Standard Bible Encyclopedia, the word "reverence" occurs as the translation of two Hebrew words, yare' and shachah. The root idea of the former is "fear." It is used to express the attitude toward God Himself. (International Standard Bible Encyclopedia). As written in the International Standard Bible Encyclopedia, in the New Testament, "reverence" occurs as the translation of three Greek words,

1. Aidos- Modesty

2. Phobeomai- Fear

3. Entrepomai-   "self-valuation   of
   inferiority," and so sets forth an attitude
   toward another of doing him honor

As observed, this word reverence whether
seen in the Old Testament or the New
Testament essentially comes to one
understanding; and that is respect. I would
like to share with you a definition that I
believe the Holy Spirit shared with me as it
concerns this word reverence. Reverence is
a reverse in behavior. It is a turning away
from wrongful actions. It is my belief that
honor towards mankind is honor towards
God. When we make the decision to treat
people with kingdom care we honor God.
We cannot say that we honor or reverence
God while treating humanity with
disrespect. I would like to take time to go
into the wonderful revelation seen in Psalm
34 in the Living Bible translation:

Psalm 34 Living Bible (TLB)

*I will praise the Lord no matter what
happens. I will constantly speak of his
glories and grace.[a] 2 I will boast of all his
kindness to me. Let all who are discouraged
take heart. 3 Let us praise the Lord together
and exalt his name.*

4 For I cried to him and he answered me! He freed me from all my fears. 5 Others too were radiant at what he did for them. Theirs was no downcast look of rejection! 6 This poor man cried to the Lord—and the Lord heard him and saved him out of his troubles. 7 For the Angel of the Lord guards and rescues all who reverence him.

8 Oh, put God to the test and see how kind he is! See for yourself the way his mercies shower down on all who trust in him. 9 If you belong to the Lord, reverence him; for everyone who does this has everything he needs. 10 Even strong young lions sometimes go hungry, but those of us who reverence the Lord will never lack any good thing.

11 Sons and daughters, come and listen and let me teach you the importance of trusting and fearing the Lord. 12 Do you want a long, good life? 13 Then watch your tongue! Keep your lips from lying. 14 Turn from all known sin and spend your time in doing good. Try to live in peace with everyone; work hard at it.

15 For the eyes of the Lord are intently watching all who live good lives, and he gives attention when they cry to him. 16 But the Lord has made up his mind to wipe out even the memory of evil men from the earth. 17 Yes, the Lord hears the good man when he calls to him for help and saves him out of all his troubles.

18 The Lord is close to those whose hearts are breaking; he rescues those who are humbly sorry for their sins. 19 The good man does not escape all troubles—he has them too. But the Lord helps him in each and every one. 20 Not one of his bones is broken.

21 Calamity will surely overtake the wicked; heavy penalties are meted out to those who hate the good. 22 But as for those who serve the Lord, he will redeem them; everyone who takes refuge in him will be freely pardoned.

Would you agree with me that this whole 34th Psalm is one that provokes the emotion of praise and adoration towards our father? As I began to read there were a few verses and points that the Holy Spirit helped me to see.

Psalms 34:7

"For the Angel of the Lord guards and rescues all who reverence him."

When we decide to reverse our adverse and obscene behavior and start to reverence our Lord as king and supreme over all, we will then see God's protection. We have got to understand that anything that hath not the spirit of God is none of his.

Romans 8:9,

But ye are not in flesh but in Spirit, if indeed God's Spirit dwell in you; but if any one has not the Spirit of Christ he is not of him.

I had a conversation with someone that made the statement, "I know that we mess up. We all mess up, but we are all God's children." I politely said to them that I disagreed with them because though we are all God's creation, we are not all God's children. We do not become a child of God until we go through spiritual rebirthing and are adopted into the royal family of the Lord Jesus Christ. This is a major deception that is leading countless "church" people to hell after they leave this earth. People have this warped mindset that God is a loving God and will not send them to hell. My thoughts on this are that yes God is love and he loves us. However, God never sends anyone to hell. We do it ourselves through ignorance and the rejection of truth when it comes. We appreciate God's grace and his tender mercies; however, it is my belief that the purpose of this grace and mercy (extension of life and the absence of deserved punishment) is so that we can have time to reverse our actions and start reverencing God as he deserves. Some people believe that because they don't shake their fist at God, curse at God or speak ill of Him that they are not disrespecting Him. The biggest dishonorable actions that can ever be done by someone are unrighteous acts which does not reflect that of being a representative of God. When we fornicate, smoke, lie, curse, cheat, etc, we are causing an offence by not honoring God. It is like what is written in the word of God that with their lips they praise me but with their hearts they dishonor. This simply means that we have people who speak well of God but live like their daddy is the devil. Holy words but demonic lifestyle. This is not reverence towards our holy God. When we have been born again by receiving His son Jesus Christ into our hearts, we then gain a benefit of having God assign an angel to our lives to guard us as well as to rescue us out of the mouth and hand of our enemies. When we are in trouble and unable to defend ourselves, we will receive the assistance of the angels. However, this scripture really helps the reader to know that the angel that God assigns to us guards us as well as rescues us. This is all in accordance with having reverence towards God.

Psalms 34:9-10

"9 If you belong to the Lord, reverence him; for everyone who does this has everything he needs. 10 Even strong young lions sometimes go hungry, but those of us who reverence the Lord will never lack any good thing."

Another benefit that comes with reverencing God is having God's favor in abundance. Reverence is the entry way into God's abundance. You will gain access into the realm of unmerited blessings from the Lord. Lack will never be your portion. God will make you sufficient in every area of your life. All that you need will be supplied for when you learn to reverence the Lord. It will be impossible for you to lack any good thing concerning you and your journey in this life. There is a saying that whatever you honor will in return honor you. How intelligent is it that out of a heart of pure love towards God that we show him our deep earnest sincere respect and as a result we receive his abundance.

Psalms 34:15

For the eyes of the Lord are intently watching all who live good lives, and he gives attention when they cry to him.

Having reverence towards God will gain you God's attention. Have you ever been in any situation where you just needed God's attention? Reverence towards God will cause one to be heard by the Lord. You do know that God does not hear a sinner's prayer except that of the prayer of repentance, right? However, David said that when he cried the Lord gave ear to him. David was a righteous vessel before the Lord and when he needed God to look on his situation, he got God's attention.

Prayer:

Father, I thank you that you are perfecting my reverence towards you. You have given me this amazing opportunity to honor and respect you. I call you Lord, Savior, Majesty, My king, forever. Help me to keep a strong reverence towards you as I live out the rest of this life on earth. I want to forever love you through my words and actions. Help me to never honor you with flattery speeches while dishonoring you with my very life. Help me to not misrepresent you by disrespecting you. Father I thank you for the grace to stay connected to you even while under mighty trials. Forever I choose to reverence you. In Jesus' name. Amen.

Epilogue

And because God is the greatest power, we shall not be defeated! As a believer, you will face many trials and tribulations. As a matter of fact, let's look at what David declared in Psalms 34:19-20:

Psalm 34:19-20 (NIV)
[19] The righteous person may have many troubles, but the Lord delivers him from them all; [20] he protects all his bones, not one of them will be broken.

There are two promises or guarantees in these verses. One promise is that in this life we will have many troubles. This is what many of God's people cannot understand or accept. They can not grasp the fact that such a loving and caring God will allow them to face hard situations which can shake their faith. However, what many do not know is that these obstacles will arise with a greater purpose, which will be seen with the natural eye. God uses the troubles of life as opportunities to invite the believer into another level of habitat with him. It is through these hardships that we learn to abide in the father and rest from all the disturbances that hit our souls. We learn how to be in trouble yet be calm while in it. We learn how to pray and seek God in order that we might learn to walk with great assurance and surety as he did, though faced with thorny and stony problems. The second promise is that God said that he would deliver us out of them all. Even as I write this I hear the Lord say to tell someone that this not only means that God will cause you to physically exit the trouble you are encountering but at some point his deliverance will cause you to elevate emotionally and mentally above whatever has arisen to encapsulate your faith. There are some of us that will go through but God will deliver us by building our infrastructure in order that we might go through these "afflictions" with great confidence and with his mighty strength. Let's look at Psalms 91:15.

Psalm 91:15 (NIV)
15 He will call on me, and I will answer him; I will be with him in trouble, I will deliver him and honor him.

I remember being given the opportunity to speak at a local church for a preaching engagement. In my study time, the Lord had asked me to look into the word deliver. So, I looked at the word but did not see anything significant in it other than the fact that it meant that God would bring one out of captivity. However, over the course of some hours, I was given some spiritual enlightenment. I saw the word chunked in this manner: DE-LIVER. I then heard the Lord ask me what DE meant. I thought DE meant to take away or to abolish. The Lord then asked me what the word LIVE meant. I then thought LIVE means life. It was then that I caught the revelation by putting the two meanings together. I got DE-LIVE = to take away life. It was then that God said, "behold I come to take the life out of whatever bondages that hold you captive." That was for a people in 2018, but I want to prophesy to someone reading this chapter that thing that has had its grip on you as to hinder or impede your progress in destiny is about to lose its life and soon after shall you begin to rise up to the paramount of your life in Jesus' mighty name. It is my prayer that you have found something encouraging in this book and that you will decide to share it with your friends, co-workers, family and even your enemies. Be encouraged to know that whatever life brings your way that you will and can overcome through the precious blood and matchless name of Jesus Christ.